ATROCIOUS BOOKS

Supplement

by
~~Serena Levi~~

Published by

~~BREADCRUMB~~

~~PRESS~~

Colebrooke Publications
~~www.breadcrumbpress.com~~

Copyright ~~Breadcrumb Press.~~
Colebrooke Publications
~~The moral rights of the author have been asserted.~~

ISBN 0952753790
978-0-9527-537-9-7

number   in an edition of

~~ISBN 0 9553269 0 7~~
~~978 0 9553269 0 5~~

List

With affectionate feelings - and in no particular order - for Claudia, Theodora, Dale, Akiko, William, Michael B., Caroline C., Annie, Emily, Oliver, James, Simone, Eliza, Julia, Louisette, Ethan, Marion, Irma, Elsa, Rose E., Shona, Lesley, Jane, Craig, Virginia, Renata, Marie-Pierre, Guadalupe, Mario, Kato, Lila, Edouard, Margaret C., Michael J., Nika, Elizabeth, Alan, Charlotte, Rena, Eleanor N., Helen D., Hetna, Dharamjit, Heston, Doreen, Helen & George, Elisabeth, Joseph, Santha, Waverly, Richard, Michel, Eleanor G., Fergus, Helen M., Antony & Araminta, Cathy, Maro, Fred, Caroline L., Robin, May, Margaret L., Oded, Madhur, Peter & Joan, George L., Louis, Helga, Yetty, Kenneth, Meera, Elizabeth, Frank, Margaret V., Rose G., Ruth, Marika, Marvin, Arto, Marcella, Alice and Mrs B. together with a number of ladies who chose to remain anonymous. And for Simon and, of course, R....

88 Danish Dishes

Hetna Dedichen. Paper-back. Copenhagen. Andr. Fred. Host & Son. 10th edition 1969.

spaghetti salad with anchovies and olives); 117 - 119 (penne con spinaci e ricotta, penne col sugo di cavolfiore); 150 - 151 (cappelletti di pesce col sugo di gamberetti continued, le lasagne coi carciofi) stained. Page 111 (spaghetti alla Nursina continued) and page 282 (pizza di scarola continued) caked with food. Page 281 buckled in consequence of the caking on page 282. Pages 160 -161 (fettuccine con le zucchine frite); 178 - 180 (pesce espada al

The Second Classic Italian Cookbook

Marcella Hazan. Hardback with dilapidated, stained and torn dust jacket. London. Jill Norman & Hobhouse Ltd. Revised and metricated edition 1982. ISBN 0 90690 3. Front Flyleaf stained. Back flyleaf stained and caked with food. Crumbs between pages 44 - 45 (pizza, pizza Margherita). Pages 46 - 47 (pizza Margherita continued); 71 (cold

salmoriglio, pesce (o carne) tra i due piatti); 182 - 187 (tonno in agrodolce alla trapanese, saraghine alla brace, gamberi dorati, umido di gamberi al pomodoro piccante) caked with food and stained.

Hungarian Cooking

Fred Macnicol. Paperback. Harmondsworth, Middlesex, England. Penguin Books Ltd. 1978. ISBN 0 14 046240 6. Pages 69 - 76 (csirkeragu continued - paradicsomsalát); 131 - 174 (curd doughs - basic dough) loose.

stained. Pages 210 - 211 (bhatura, roghni roti, roghni nan) caked with flour. Whole held together with elastic band.

Indian Cooking

Dharamjit Singh. Paperback. Harmondworth, Middlesex, England. Penguin Book Ltd. 1970. Covers missing. Spine frayed. Book split in two at pages 46 - 47 (mhaans turrcarri sadah, mhaans turrcarri kahsta, gurdakupura turrcarri). Pages 189 - 190 (baingan bhurta continued, seekhi baingan, tamattar bhurta, bandhgobi turrcarri, bandhgobi parcha)

Simca's Cuisine.

Simone Beck. Paperback. New York. Vintage Books. 1976. Covers stained, front and back.

The Joy of Chinese Cooking

Doreen Yen Hung Feng. Paperback. London. Faber and Faber. 1964. Front cover missing. Spine frayed. Book split in two at pages 110 - 110 (poultry). Front pages dog eared. Pages 107 - 110 (keh jup chow haah kow, yang chow haah kow, dow see loong haah, poultry); 125 (ging jeung ngaap); 136 - 137 (chaah sieu, hoong sieu jüh yook); 165 - 211 (sieu ngaap jook - festival of the moon) stained. Whole held together with elastic band.

Chinese Food

Kenneth Lo. Paperback. Harmondsworth, Middlesex, England. Penguin Books Ltd. 1972. Covers stained and dog eared. Loose bundles of pages front of book through page 86 (sweet and sour pork) and at pages 87 - 116 (barbecued spare ribs - sliced steak in oyster sauce). Loose page at 117 - 118 (sliced steak in oyster sauce continued, quick sweet and sour spare ribs, quick-fried crab in aromatic oil). Pages 85 - 88 (sweet and sour pork, barbecued spare ribs); 116 - 117 (pork and watercress soup, sliced steak in oyster sauce, quick-fried sweet and sour spare ribs) stained.

The Best of Eliza Acton

Elizabeth Ray (editor). Paperback. Harmonds- worth, Middlesex, England. Penguin Books Limited. 1974. Stained back cover.

The World's Best Recipes

Marvin Small. Paperback. New York. Pocket Books, Inc. 4th printing November, 1962. Covers missing. Gen. dilapidated.

The Bean Book

Rose Elliot. Paperback. Great Britain. Fontana. 5th impression January 1982.

The Food and Cooking of Russia

Lesley Chamberlain. Paper- back. Harmondsworth, Middlesex, England. Penguin Books. 1983. Cracked spine. Gen. dilapidated.

Mediterranean Seafood

Alan Davidson. Paperback. London. The Penguin Group. 2nd edition, 1981. ISBN 0 14 046804 8. Pages 73 - 94 slightly crumpled. Pages 95 - 112 damaged bottom corner (red mullet, sciaenid fish etc, meagre, blue fish, scad, horse mackerel, amberjack, pilot fish, pompano, dolphin fish, ray's bream, wrasses and kindred fish, cuckoo wrasse, wrasse corkwing).

English Food

Jane Grigson. Paperback. London. The Penguin Group. 1993. ISBN 0 14 027324 7.

Frida's Fiestas: Recipes and Reminiscences of Life with Frida Kahlo

Guadalupe Rivera and Marie-Pierre Colle. Kenneth Krabbenhoft (translator, text) and Olga Rigsby (translator, recipes). Hardback with dust jacket. New York. Clarkson Potter. ISBN 0 517 59235 5. Leaflet from Piano Keyboard acting as bookmark at pages 41 - 3 (red hominey stew from Jalisco, flan).

The Mushroom Feast

Jane Grigson. Paperback. Harmondsworth, Middlesex, England. Penguin Books Ltd. 1978. ISBN 0 14 045273 2. Covers frayed, back and front. Pages i - xv stained (note of author, title, dedication, table of contents, introduction). Index pages xv - xx (poultry continued - Yuan Mei, her bêche-de-mer gourmet) and end pages dog eared. Gen. friable and dilapidated.

Spices, Salt and Aromatics in the English Kitchen

Elizabeth David. Paperback. Harmondsworth, Middlesex, England. Penguin Books Ltd. Reprinted1971. Pages 277 - 279 stained (index: salted almonds - zucchini). Back cover marked and badly stained.

In Search of Plenty: A History of Jewish Food

Oded Schwartz. Paperback. London. Kyle Cathie Ltd. 1992. ISBN 1 85626 099 2.

The Book of Latin American Cooking

Elisabeth Lambert Ortiz. Paperback. Harmondsworth, Middlesex, England. The Penguin Group. 1985. ISBN 0 14 046922 2.

The Classic Italian Cookbook

Marcella Hazan. Paperback. London. Macmillan London Limited. Revised and metricated edition 1980. Covers stained and dog eared. Spine broken at pages 16 - 17 (cutting tools, food processors, odds and ends). Pages 84 - 85 (spaghettini con le melanzane, spaghettini alle vongole); 109 - 112 bolognese sauce, tagliatelle alla bolognese,

fettuccine all'Alfredo, paglia e fieno alla ghiotta) stained. Spine broken at pages 176 - 177, both pages stained (polenta al burro e formaggio, polenta fritta, polenta col gorgonzola). Pages 244 - 247 (fagioli dall'occhio con salsicce, coda alla vaccinara, trippa alla parmigiana) stained. First four pages and pages 403 - to end (hors d'oeuvres continued - zuppa di vongole vellutata) dog eared.

New Indian Cooking

Meera Taneja. Paperback. Great Britain. Fontana Paperbacks. 1983. ISBN 0 00 0636450 0.

Mastering the Art of French Cooking. Volume I

Simone Beck, Louisette Bertholle, Julia Child. London. The Penguin Group. 14th reprinting 1988. Cover tattered. Spine broken at pages 226 - 227 (croquettes, chaussons) and pages 638 - 639 (bavarois à l'orange continued, bavarois au chocolat).

Cooking the Hungarian Way

Kato Frank. Paperback. London. Paul Hamlyn. 1963. Covers tattered and stained.

Madhur Jaffrey's Indian Cookery

Madhur Jaffrey. Paperback. London. The British Broadcasting Corporation. 1982. Inside cover stained. Pages 66 (Tandori-style chicken) and 170 (Gujerati carrot salad) stained.

River Café Cook Book Easy

Rose Gray and Ruth Rogers. Hardback with dust jacket. London. Ebury Press. ISBN 009 188464 0. Bookmark from The Guardian book service at pages 162 - 163 (duck with tomato).

Pocket Beer Guide

Michael Jackson. Paperback. London. J Sainsbury plc. 1996. ISBN 1 870694 19 9.

The Cuisine of Hungary

George Lang. Hardback with stained dust jacket. New York. Bonanza Books. 1971. ISBN 0 517 16963 0. Inscription flyleaf: R$4 95C. Spine broken at pages 314 - 315 (stuffed morels continued - lescó). Broken spine and stains at pages 390 - 391 (my Mother's cherry cake, corn cake as in Transdanubia, sheet cake filled with apples). Page 393 (latticed chocolate pite) stained.

Jane Grigson's Vegetable Book

Jane Grigson. Hardback. London. Michael Joseph. 1978. ISBN 0 7181 1675 5. Spine torn. Flyleaf inscription: 6 - 75. Birthday card from Florence acting as bookmark between pages 122 - 123 (gratin of brussel sprouts continued, brabant purée, brussel sprout soup). Birthday card from Valerie and Geoffrey acting as bookmark between pages pages 420 - 421 (East Craftsbury pumpkin or squash soup, roast pumpkin, fried pumpkin, American baked pumpkin). Folded transparent carrier-bag acting as bookmark between pages 382 - 383 (Spanish pepper soup continued, peperonata, pipérade basquaise, Basque pepper and egg tarts). Dedication page; pages 94 - 95 (Russian borshch continued, simplified variations, beetroot stock); 178 (cauliflower with parsley butter, cauliflower parmesan, red hot cauliflower, cauliflower in the Sicilian style); 221 (how to choose and prepare Chinese leaf continued, stir-fried Chinese leaf); 290 (Welsh lamb with laver continued) stained and caked with food. Debris in the crevice between pages 480 - 481 (spring and winter greens). Corner of page 31 (how to buy and prepare asparagus) sharply turned under. Pages 49 - 51 (sweet-sour aubergine Spanish style, parmagiana di cauliflower and green bean salad, Greek cauli-flower) stained.

The Magimix and Food Processor Cookery Book

Marika Tenison Hanbury. Hardback with stained dust jacket. Isleworth, Middlesex, Uk. Icte Ltd. 5th impression 1978. Flyleaf and title page stained. Pages 146 - 147 (making sauces in your Magimix food processor, Magimix mayonnaise) caked with food.

An Omelette and a Glass of Wine

Elizabeth David. Hardback. Plastic covered dust jacket with area torn out. London. Jill Norman. 2nd reprinting 1985. Sticker on back: HALE-net £10.95. Inside cover scarred with pasted card and paper. 1st page torn out almost completely. Title page inscription: 80p. Corner irregularly torn out pages 1 - 8. Page 199 (English lemon curd) stained.

Cooking the Greek Way

Maro Duncan. Paperback. London. Paul Hamlyn. 1964. Pages 197 - 198 (skordalia, ladoxitho, saltsa domata) burned.

Marcella's Italian Kitchen

Marcella Hazan. Hardback with dust jacket. New York. Alfred A. Knopf. 1987. ISBN 0 394 59892 0. Page 56 (torta di spinaci continued, la "Turta" di spinaci e riso) stained. Pages 57 - 58 (zucchine ripiene di tonno) buckled and marked in a circular pattern.

Marcella Cucina

Marcella Hazan. Hardback with dust jacket. London and Basingstoke. Macmillan General Books. 1997. ISBN 0 333 62734 2. Good condition.

The Jewish Manual: Information on Jewish and Modern Cookery with a Collection of Valuable Recipes and Hints Relating to the Toilette

A Lady (editor). Chaim Raphael, introduction. Paperback. Cold Spring, New York. NightinGale Books. Facsimile of 1st edition (1846) 1983.

Cooking with Pomiane

Edouard de Pomiane. Hardback with torn dust jacket. London. The Cookery Club. 1969.

Picnic

Claudia Roden. Paperback, Harmondsworth, Middlesex, England. Penguin Books Ltd. 1982. ISBN 0 14 046 323 2. Covers slightly dog eared and slightly stained. Loose pages 107 - 108 (Jane Grigson's kipper flan, leek pie, Jane Grigson's raised pie) and 373 - 378 (index courgettes tarts - oil types). Spine broken at pages 172 - 173 (hunting feasts continued, lampries in Ceylon). Loose sections

pages 173 - 196 (a letter from Malkanthi Scott - an open wood fire continued) and 197 - 240 (charcoal fires – mixed grill). Whole held together with elastic band.

Mrs Beeton's Cookery Book

Mrs Beeton née Mayson. Hardback. London. Ward, Lock & Co, Limited. New edition 1901.

Chinese Regional Cookery

Margaret Leeming and May Huang Man-hui. Paperback. London. Rider & Company Ltd. 1983. ISBN 0 09 150981 5.

Menus for Grills: Le Creuset

Yetty Line. Paperback booklet. Brussels. Editions Ediar. 1976.

The Settlement Cook-book: The Way to a Man's Heart

No bibliographic data. Hardback. Front cover detached; back cover missing. Front pages missing. Pages missing page 607 on. Gen. friable and dilapidated. Newspaper clipping acting as bookmark: stuffed eggplant with cheese; sausage and macaroni casserole; creamed spinach.

The Rituals of Dinner

Margaret Visser. Hardback with dust jacket. New York. Grove Weidenfeld. 1991. ISBN 0 8021 1116 5. Mint condition.

The Book of Tofu: Food for Mankind

William Shurtleff & Akiko Aoyagi. Paperback. New York. Ballantine Books. Revised edition 1979. ISBN 0 345 27809 7.

Vegetarian Dishes from the Middle East

Arto der Haroutunian. Paperback. London. Century Publishing. 1984. ISBN 0 7126 0320 4.

A Taste of the West Country in Food and in Pictures

Theodora Fitzgibbon. Paperback. London. Pan Books. 1975.

Food for Free: A Guide to the Edible Wild Plants of Britain

Richard Mabey. Paperback. Great Britain. Fontana. 1975.

Slimming with Magimix

Marika Hanbury Tenison. Spiral Bound. Isleworth, Middx. ICTC Ltd.

The Magimix Food Preparation Machine Information: Instruction & Recipe Book

Marika Hanbury Tenison. Paperback booklet. France. Information sheet inside: electric ice cream machines.

The Chinese Cookbook

Craig Claiborne and Virginia Lee. London. Paperback. Andre Deutsch Limited. 1973.

Cuisine Gourmande

Michel Guérard. Edited and adapted by Caroline Conran. Paperback. London. Macmillan London. 1978.

The New York Times Cookbook

Craig Claiborne. Hardback. New York. Harper & Row. 1966. Covers coming away. Page 291 (chicken livers en brochette); 292 (chicken livers Madeira, chicken liver timbales); 391 (golden buck, tomato rabbit, caraway macaroni rabbit); 578 (almond blancmange); 579 (coconut blancmange, coconut pudding); 621 (marble cake, Norwegian mocha cake) stained. Pages 332 - 333 (Mexican rabbit, gougère, cheese and rice avocados); 589 - 594 (queen of puddings, steamed sponge pudding, Elizabeth Borton de Treviño's best pudding, apple soufflé with lemon-nutmeg sauce, chocolate soufflé, lemon soufflé, soufflé Rothschild, grenadine Rothschild) very seriously stained.

Ice Cream, Sorbets, Frozen Yogourts, Parfaits, Bombes and More

Shona Crawford Poole. Paperback. Conrad Octopus. ISBN 1 84091 173 5.

Jane Grigson's Fruit Book

Jane Grigson. Paperback. Harmondsworth, Middlesex, England. Penguin Books. 1983. ISBN 0 14 046 535 9. Covers stained, front and backed. Whole dog eared. Blank slip of paper acting as bookmark at pages 60 - 61 (banana fritters, Octave Uzanne's bananas, plum blossom and snow). Pages 364 - 366 (tsimmes, oxtail with prunes and cornmeal fritters) wrinkled.

Ices: The Definitive Guide

Caroline Liddell & Robin Weir. Hardback. London. Grub Street. Fifth reprinting 1999. ISBN 1 898697 26 4. Leaflet inside: Gelato Chef 2000. Newspaper clipping inside: Heston Blumenthal's orange and ginger water ice and his blackcurrent sorbet.

Danish Cooking: A Penguin Handbook

Nika Standen Hazelton. Paperback. Harmondsworth, Middlesex, England. Penguin Books. Published with revisions 1967.

Nose to Tail Eating: A Kind of British Cooking

Fergus Henderson. Paperback. London. Pan Books. 2000. ISBN 0 330 48448 6.

English Bread and Yeast Cookery

Elizabeth David. Hardback with tattered dust jacket. London. Allan Lane, Penguin Books Ltd. Reprinted, 1978. ISBN 0 7130 1026 7. Flyleaf inscription: 4.30.

North Atlantic Seafood

Alan Davidson. Paperback. Wright's Lane, London. Penguin Books. ISBN 0 14 046815 3.

The Book of Jewish Food: An Odyssey from Samarkand to New York

Claudia Roden. Hardback with dust jacket. New York. Alfred A. Knopf. 1997. ISBN 0 394 53258 9. Mint Condition.

The Cooking of the Middle East: A Sainsbury Cookbook

Claudia Roden. Paperback. London. Martin Books. 2nd Impression 1992. ISBN 0 85941 819 7.

An Invitation to Indian Cooking

Madhur Jaffrey. Paperback. Harmondsworth, Middlesex, England. Penguin Books. 1978. Covers tattered.

Summer Cooking

Elizabeth David. Paperback. Harmondsworth, Middlesex, England. Penguin Books. 12th reprinting of enlarged revised version 1978. ISBN 0 14 046 100 0.

Leipoldt's Cape Cookery

C. Louis Leipoldt. Hardback with dust jacket. Cape Town. W.J. Flesch & Partners. Reprinted 1983. ISBN 0 949989 15 0. Sticky yellow slip on front cover: Friend - Good. Newspaper clipping (Marinades and Memories by Emily Green) between pages 76 - 78 (meat bredie). Good condition.

The American Heritage Cookbook

Helen McNulty (recipes editor), Eleanor Noderer (associate recipes editor), Helen Duprey Bullock (historical foods consultant). Paperback. Harmondsworth, Middlesex, England. Penguin Books Ltd. 1967. Covers stained and creased. Back cover missing bottom corner. Title page, table of contents and preface stained. Pages 243 - 253 (Russian salad - sweet pickled peaches) creased at bottom. Pages 253 - 258 (Albemarle peach chutney - New Orleans calas) creased at top. Pages 249 - 253 (sun-cooked strawberry jam, candied cranberries, cranberry sauce, spiced crab apples, apple sauce, Albemarle peach chutney, sweet pickled peaches); 255 - 271 (ginger pears, carrot pickles, Yankee tomato relish, tomato ketchup, tomato preserves, pickled jerusalem artichokes, New Orleans calas, a nun's sigh, fruit fritters, olykoeks, fastnachts, pannequaiques, strawberry shortcake, blueberry shortcake, plums in wine jelly, ambrosia, frozen plum pudding, salpiçon of fruits, bananas flambés, spiced peaches in brandy, hazelnut bavarian cream, blancmange, Cape Cod berry grunt, peach cobbler, Louisa May Alcott's apple slump, down East apple brown Betty, apple pandowdy) stained. Pages 289 - 292 (pastry for pie crust, lemon meringue pie, Key lime pie, apple pie) caked with food, stained and crumpled. Pages 253 - end (Roman punch on) stained top corner. Pages 269 - end (index: grilled trout) dog eared bottom corner. Gen. friable and dilapidated.

Secrets of the Master Chefs of China

By the editors of China Pictorial, the People's Republic of China. Hardback with slightly damaged dust jacket. Newton Abbot and London. David & Charles. 1983. Good condition.

The Cooking of India

Santha Rama Rau and the editors of Time-Life Books. Hardback. New York. Time-Life Books. 1969. Good condition.

Recipes: The Cooking of India

Spiral Bound. Covers stained. Label front cover: Savile Book Shop, 3236 P St., N.W. (and in ms) Time Life Cooking of India 7.95.

The Country Kitchen

Jocasta Innes. Hardback with dust jacket. Great Britain. Weidenfeld and Nicholson Ltd. Small food blotch at page 223 (pickles and chutneys).

American Cooking

Hard board folder with rucked plastic covering. Inside sticker: #4.95.

American Cooking

Dale Brown and the editors of Time-Life Books. Hardback. Time-Life International (Nederland) B.V. Reprinted 1974. Fair condition but covers dirty.

Recipes: American Cooking

Spiral bound. Reprinted 1974. Small stain page 85 (clover leaf rolls, baking powder biscuits).

The Cooking of Italy

Hard board folder with soiled plastic covering.

The Cooking of Italy

Waverly Root and the editors of Time-Life Books. Hardback. Time-Life International (Nederland) N.V.. 1970. Slightly stained first page.

Recipes: The Cooking of Italy

Margaret Costa (consultant). Spiral Bound. Time-Life International (Nederland) N.V.. Covers grubby.

American Cooking: The Melting Pot

James P. Shenton, Angelo M. Pellegrini, Dale Brown, Israel Shenker, Peter Wood and the editors of Time-Life Books. Hardback. New York. Time-Life Books. 1971. Newspaper clipping (lobster with a chocolate sauce, sorbet au cacao, amaretto soufflé, Dum's chocolate pudding) between pages 62 - 63 (stuffed whole cabbage with sauerkraut).

Recipes: American Cooking: The Melting Pot

Spiral Bound. New York. Time-Life Books. 1971. Back cover slightly soiled.

The South African Culinary Tradition with 167 Authentic Recipes

Renata Coetzee. Hardback with dust jacket. Cape Town. C. Struik Publishers. Fifth Impression 1988. Mint condition.

Great Dinners from Life

Eleanor Graves. Hardback. New York. Time-Life Books. Reprinted 1970. All pages buckled. Page 239 torn (index: meat and fish sauces).

The Sunday Times Guide to the World's Best Food

Michael Bateman. Caroline Conran. Oliver Gillie. Hardback with dust jacket. London. Hutchinson & Co. (Publishers) Ltd. 1981. Dust jacket stained. Crease on second page.

The Cooking of Russia

Hard board folder with plastic covering. Slightly soiled. Back cover rucked. Sticker inside (crossed out in pencil): £ 5.95. Pencilled inscription inside: 3-75.

The Cooking of Russia

Helen and George Papashvily and the editors of Time-Life Books. Time-Life International (Nederland) B.V.. Fourth printing 1975. Pre-title page and two back pages buckled.

Recipes: The Cooking of Russia

Spiral bound. Covers slightly soiled.

The Cooking of Vienna's Empire

Hard board folder with plastic covering. Covers slightly soiled and back cover yellowing. Pencilled inscription inside board: 4.60.

The Cooking of Vienna's Empire

Joseph Wechsberg and the editors of Time-Life Books. Hardback. Time-Life International (Nederland) N.V.. Fourth English printing 1974. Page 193 (bublanina, haselnusstorte) stained.

Recipes: The Cooking of Vienna's Empire

Spiral Bound. Time-Life International (Nederland) N.V.. Fourth English printing, 1976. Covers slightly soiled. Page 6 (liptavsky syr) buckled.

and dilapidated. Given as a gift to Martha Hellion, June 2004.

The Alice B. Toklas Cook Book

Alice B. Toklas. Paperback. Harmondsworth, Middlesex. Penguin Books Ltd. 1962. Covers creased, dirty and dog eared. Spine frayed. Back cover separated from the rest of volume. All pages dog eared. All pages missing after page 336 (index: white beans, browned-in-the-oven white beans). Page 336 torn. Whole held together with elastic band. Gen. friable

Charcuterie and French Pork Cookery

Jane Grigson. Paperback. Harmondsworth, Middlesex, England. Penguin Books Ltd. Reprinted 1975. ISBN 0 14 046 1. Covers creased. Back cover caked with food, inside and out. Title page loose. Spine broken at page 176 (petit salé) with pages 177 - 178 (petit salé aux petits pois, petits pois au lard, petit salé au choux, petit salé aux pois secs) loose and creased. Loose

bundles of pages at 179 - 232 (pommes de terre au lard, petit salé au poireaux, petit salé aux pommes, petit salé aux champignons, côtes de porc sautées à la gasconne, côtes de porc à la bayonnaise) and at 233 - 260 (côtes de porc au vin blanc, côtes de porc à la charcutiere, pieds de porc vinaigrette, pig's trotters with onion sauce) detached. Whole held together with elastic band. Gen. friable and dilapidated.

Jane Grigson's Fish Book

Jane Grigson. Paperback. London. The Penguin Group. 1993. ISBN 0 14 046929 X.

Italian Food

Elizabeth David. Paperback. Harmondsworth, Middlesex, England. 7th reprinting, 1969. ISBN 0 14 046 098 5. Covers wrinkled and stained. Pages 351 (index: Piedmont - olive oil in cooking) to end dog eared. Loose page from French Provincial Cooking (glossary of fish names: kipper - king whitings) acting as book-mark between pages 172 (pesce alla griglia) and 173 (pesce in cartoccio).

Mastering the Art of French Cooking, Volume Two

Julia Child and Simone Beck. Hardback. New York. A Borzoi Book Published by Alfred A. Knopf, Inc. Sixth printing March 1973. Covers soiled. Pages 367 - 369 (courgettes etuvées à la crème continued, courgettes gratinées mornay, courgettes en persillade gratinées, courgettes en pistouille, courgettes rapées,

courgettes rapées sautées); 379 - 384 (chou farci, feuilles de chou farcies); 395 - 397 (pommes Anna continued, pommes de terre sarladaise, gallette de pommes de terre au fromage); 401 (pommes duchesse continued); 403 (galettes de pommes de terre farcie); 405 (purée freneuse); 411 (salade de poivrons provençale); 420 (langue de chats continued); 422 - 423 (le Kilimanjaro, glace au chocolat pralinée continued, mousse glacée pralinée aux noix - appareil à bombe); 427 (le Saint-Cyr glacé continued); 436 - 437 (flan aux prunes, clafouti aux prunes, pommes soufflées calvados); 537 (illustrations of various kitchen implements) stained. Pages 370 - 378 (tian de courgettes au riz, timbale de courgettes, stuffed zucchini, courgettes farcies aux amandes, courgettes farcies au riz et aux poivrons, stuffed onions); 398 - 400 (tourte limousine, pommes duchesse); 425 - 426 (le Saint-Cyr glacé) buckled. Pages 406 - 407 (la purée chateaux en Suede, petits navets sautés en garniture); 416 - 419 (mousse à l'abricot glacée, bombe glacé à l'abricot, mousse aux fraises ou aux framboises glacés, coupelles, langues de chats) caked with food. Pages 438 - 439 (pommes soufflées calvados continued) stained, stuck together and torn where prised apart. A hole in page 439 - 440 (poires meringuées au sabayon) results. Pages 487 - 494 (le genoise electrique, crème au beurre à la meringue Italienne, gateau aux noix le Saint-André, la Charlotte Africaine) badly stained and buckled. Page 404 (gratin de potiron d'Arpajon) marked with sticky yellow slip.

James Beard's American Cookery

James Beard. Hardback. Boston and Toronto. Little, Brown and Company. 1972. Spine torn towards back. Covers soiled. Spine broken at pages 18 - 19 (Scotch eggs, chili con carne, sausages with cocktails). Page 19 in addition is stained. Pages 671 - 672 (pumpkin or squash spice cake, double apple cake or cupcakes, apple sauce cake); page 674 (pork cake, mayonnaise cake) buckled and dog eared. Page 673 (raw apple bread or cake, fresh carrot cake); pages 675 - 678 (chocolate or chocolate caramel potato cake, fudge cake, chocolate custard or devil's food cake, sweet chocolate cake, crazy cake or crazy mixed-up cake, red devil's food cake, red velvet cake, chocolate upside-down cake) dog eared, buckled and stained. 678 - 679 (roulade Léontine or chocolate roll continued, chocolate soufflé, sponge roll or sponge layer); 703 - 705 (rolled cookies, sandbakelse, sand tarts, Scotch shortbread, snickerdoodles, spekulaas); 709- 713 (stick candy cookies, almond pretzels, Chinese almond cookies, anise caps, apple or prune or apricot or pineapple sauce cookies, fresh apple cookies, bourbon or sherry or rum or brandy balls or walnut spirit balls, brown sugar or tan or pecan kisses, brownies, carrot cookies, cherubs or honeymoon bars or dream bars or lover's morsels, sweet chocolate or chocolate chunk or chocolate chip or Toll House cookies); page 717 (ginger-bread men, gingersnaps); 719 (lebkucken); 721 (mincemeat cookies, molasses cookies); pages 723 - 726 (apple brown Betty, apple Charlotte, apple dumplings, apple pan dowdy, Charleston pudding, blueberry grunt, huckleberry dumplings, prune whip, vanilla pudding, old-fashioned blancmange, the Coach House bread and butter

pudding, colonial cheese pudding); 783-784 (a good whole-wheat bread, whole-grain bread, health bread, Anadama bread); 792-797 (brown bread, Jeanne Owen's cornbread, gingerbread, baking powder biscuits, buttermilk biscuits, simple muffins, cornmeal muffins, bran muffins, popovers, basic griddle cakes, buttermilk pancakes, Henri Thiele's German pancakes); 841-843 (reading list and sources) buckled and stained. Pages 811 - 812 (tuna fish

sandwich, salmon sandwich, sardine sandwich, anchovy sandwich, lobster or shrimp or crab meat sandwiches, egg sandwich, cucumber sandwich, tomato sandwich) buckled and with bottom corner folded over towards the front. Pages 813 - 821 (onion sandwich, cheese sandwich, cottage cheese sandwich, hero or grinder or submarine or sub sandwich, picnic or lunch box or tea sandwiches, dainty sandwiches, sandwich

loaves, six-minute strawberry preserves, sunshine strawberry preserves, apricot pineapple conserve, fruit butters, uncooked frozen jams, watermelon rind pickles) bottom corner folder over towards the front page. Page 718 (hermits, jumbles); pages 785 - 786 (rye bread, hot-water bread, Swedish limpa, Middle Eastern bread); 798 - 801 (waffles, cake doughnuts, raised doughnuts, crullers, fried rice cakes) buckled. Pages 754 - 756 (figs with

prosciutto, roast figs Mrs. Crowen, gooseberry fool, grapes with brown sugar and sour cream, frosted grapes, broiled grapefruit, flavoured grapefruit sections, poached ground-cherries) stained. Pages 677, 704, 717, 797, 813 and 840 - 841 are also caked with food. Crumbs between pages 710 - 711.

Cooking the Spanish Way

Elsa Behrens. Paperback. London. Paul Hamlyn. 1962. Cover stained, torn and detached from pages. Paper strip stuck between pages 96 - 97 (budín de merluza con mayonesa, lenguado a la crema, pastel de pescado económico). Top corners curling pages 195 - end (salsa de pan frito, salsa muselina on). Whole held together with elastic band.

375 - 376 loose, stained, torn and food-caked. Page from unidentified cookbook (index of recipes: pies and tarts - quince and orange pie) serving as place-marker between pages 248 - 249 (stuffed tomatoes, basic tomato sauce, pizza-iola sauce). Whole held together with elastic band. Gen. friable and dilapidated.

Good Things

Jane Grigson. Paperback. Harmondsworth, Middlesex, England. Penguin Books Ltd. 1973. Covers missing. Pages 373 - 374 (index of recipes: grape brandy - pineapple liqueur) loose and all pages after page 374 missing. Pre-title page missing bottom corner and with a fragment torn out. Title page - end of introduction dog eared. Caked food on page 304 (strawberries and cream, coeur à la crème). Page

The Book of the Sausage

Antony and Araminta Hippisley Coxe. Paperback. London. Pan Books.1978. ISBN 0 330 25417 9. Pages 109 - 150 (Leoni sausage - saucisses de Strasbourg) in a separate bundle because spine has cracked between pages 108 (leberstreichwurst, leber-wurst) and 151 (saucisse de Thann, saucisse de Toulouse).

The Chocolate Book

Helga Rubinstein. Paperback. London. The Penguin Group. 1982. ISBN 0 14 046888 9. Covers tattered. Pencilled inscription on flyleaf: 493, £5.95 (crossed out), £2.50v substituted.

Mexican Cooking at the Academy

Susan Lammers, editor. Vicki Barrios Schley and Angelo Villa, writers. Paperback. California Culinary Academy Series published by the staff of the Cole Group. 1993. ISBN 1 56426 040 2. Sticker on back cover: Fountain Press £ 8.95. Page 29 (sopa de fideo, hearty pozole dinner, pozole) stained. Glossy leaflet from La Mexicana Quality Foods Ltd (Aztec Pie, burritos)

acting as bookmark between pages 34 - 35 (menudo, frijoles chorros, sopa de papas y chile verde, sopa de melón escribe, sopa de tortilla, arroz a la Mexicana) and another identical leaflet (caked with food) between pages 58 - 59 (tacos, taquitos). Folded plastic bag which once held 8 stoneground corn tortillas made by La Mexicana acting as bookmark between pages 102 - 103 (coctel de abulon, coctel

de mariscos, abulon en escabeche, camarones escorpionados con chile rojo, ensalada de pescado, ensalada de camarones, ensalada de queso asadero).

Home on the Range: A Culinary History of the American West

Cathy Luchetti. Paperback. New York. Villard Books. 1993. ISBN 0 679 74484 3. Front cover slightly soiled and top corner bent. First page - page xxviii bent at top corner. Pages xxix - xxx top corner creased.

Seafood: A Connoisseur's Guide and Cookbook

Alan Davidson and Charlotte Knox. Hardback with dust jacket and integral ribbon. London. Mitchell Beazley. ISBN 0 855 33 752 4. Caked food front flap of dust jacket. Slight soiling flyleaf. Otherwise in good condition.

Japanese Cooking

Peter and Joan Martin. Paperback. Harmondsworth, Middlesex, England. Penguin Books Ltd. 1972. ISBN 0 14 046 175 2. Covers creased.

French Provincial Cooking

Elizabeth David. Paperback. Harmondsworth, Middlesex, England. Penguin Books Ltd. Ninth reprinting of revised edition with revisions 1978. ISBN 0 14 046 099 3. Covers creased and crumpled with front corners missing. Inscription on flyleaf: 9 S. Beginning - page 19 and page 548 - end dog eared. Pages 349 - 350 (aïoli - la bourride de Charles Bérot) loose.   Pages 351 - 352

missing. Book broken into two parts: the first ends at page 348 (la bouillabaisse des pêcheurs continued). The second starts at page 353 (morue aux tomates, morue en rayte). Whole held together with elastic band. Gen. friable and dilapidated.

A Book of Middle Eastern Food

Claudia Roden. Paperback. Harmondsworth, Middlesex, England. Penguin Books Ltd. 1970. Covers creased. Front inside cover stained. Back cover disengaging from body of book. From beginning through page 70 (title, dedication, contents, acknowledgements, introduction, a bowl of fresh herbs, an egg hors d'oeuvre, wara einab, hot stuffed vine leaves, cold

stuffed vine leaves, aubergine purée, aubergine purée with yoghourt, fried aubergines with yoghourt, gebna beida, fried or grilled cheese, fried liver pieces, onions with vinegar, brain salad, tahina cream salad, hummus bi tahina, baba ghanoush, tahina bil fessih, ta'amia or falafel, artichokes hearts stewed in oil, koftit ferakh, dukkah, aubergine slices stuffed with cream cheese, batarkeh, taramasalata, midye tavasi, blehat samak, cold mussel

plaki, carmel avocado purée, avocado purée with tuna, avacado purée with cream cheese); pages 113 - 181 (tyropitta, kotopitta, large meat pie, bstilla, tagine malsouka, lahma bi ajeen, ataïf with cheese, hamud, beid bi lamoun, melokhia, havuç çorbasi, ful nabed soup, lentil soup, spinach and lentil soup, Turkish spinach soup, yellow split pea soup, haricot bean soup, labaneya, cold cucumber and yogourt soup, Turkish yoghourt soups, tutmaj, eshkeneh

shirazi, rich meat and vegetable soup, beef and puréed vegetable soup, meat ball soup, Armenian meat soup with burghul, düǧvün çorbasi, fata, shorbet el samak, beid masluq, beid mutajjan, beid hamine, hard-boiled eggs, deep-fried eggs, beid masus, scrambled eggs with vinegar, beid bi tom, beid bi tamatem, beid bi gebna maqlia, fried eggs with chicken liver, chakchouka, çalbir, eggah bi eish wa kousa, eggah bi kousa, eggah bi ful akhdar, eggah bi betingan, eggah bi korrat, eggah bi sabaneh, eaggah bi lahma, eggah bi ferakh wa rishta, ojja bil mergaz, eggah bi mokh, kukuye sabsi, kuku sibzamini, omlettes, herb omelette, samak maqli, fried fish with cousbareia sauce, beid bi lamoun, khall wakardal, zemino sauce for fried fish, fish fried in butter, sardines in the Algerian manner, deep-fried or grilled small fish, small red mullet with garlic, blehat samak, fish in olive oil, fish plaki, boiled or poached fish, fish baked in the oven, samak tarator, samak malqlu bi khall wa rahshi, uskumru dolmasu, sayyadiah); 301 - 304 (aubergines, tomatoes and green peppers in oil continued, turlu, moussaka, kousa bi gebna, hünkâr beǧendi, artichoke hearts and broad beans in oil) stained. Pages 47, 49 and 66 also caked with food. Pages 65 - 58 and 113 - 114 also dog eared as are pages 391 - end (apricot pudding, orange jelly - †not for sale in the U.S.A.). There is a small triangular piece cut away at the top of pages 151-156. Gen. friable and dilapidated.

The Cooking of Greece and Turkey: A Sainsbury Cookbook

Rena Salaman. Paperback. London. Martin Books. Third Impression 1990. ISBN 0 85941 487 6.

Joy of Cooking

Irma S. Rombauer and Marion Rombauer Becker. Hardback with two integral ribbons. Other bibliographic data missing. The boards forming the front and back covers have become detached from the volume and the spine-binding is missing. The boards are soiled and stained, and the paper on the inside is torn. Beginning pages - page 2 (forward and guide, table of contents - the foods we

Cooking the Polish Way

Lila Kowalska. Paperback. London Paul Hamlyn Limited. 1964. Covers tattered. Slight staining pages 163-171 (yeast coffee cake, babka made with pumpkin, crumble cake, coffee cake with crumble top, Albert biscuits, almond cookies, apples in dressing gowns, chocolate slices, chocolate slices with apples, choux pastry for cream buns or éclairs).

eat through about accessory factors in food) dog eared top and bottom, torn and stained. Pages 833 - 838 (index: ravioli - sausage) dog eared top and bottom, torn and coming away from volume at the bottom. Pages 3 - 22 (the foods we eat continued through party dinner menus: tomatoes stuffed with crab meat salad, fillet of beef with marchand de vin sauce, franconia or browned potatoes, stuffed baked artichokes, ricotta cheese

pie; 827 - 832 (liver pâté - hot sauce ravigote) dog eared top and bottom. These pages are also coming loose from the volume at the bottom. Pages 15 - 18 (about buffet service continued - breakfast menus: sliced rounds of honeydew melon filled with raspberries, ham and potato cakes with eggs) are also beginning to work loose from the volume. Pages 23 - 37 (party dinner menus: bouillabaisse, mixed salad greens with French dressing, French bread,

assorted fruit); 215 - 216 (cornmeal pancakes, crisp corn flapjacks, rice cornmeal griddle cakes, oatmeal griddle cakes, buckwheat cakes, onion griddle cakes, rice flour griddle cakes, waffles); 677 - 678 dog eared at the top. Pages 51 - 54 (Tom and Jerry in quantity, mulled wine or negus in quantity, wassail, hot buttered rum - Christmas canapés, zoo sandwiches, sandwich loaves, tarts and tartlets for canapés); pages 813 - 8 32 (index: foods we heat -

meringue toppings) dog eared at the bottom. Pages 109 - 114 (fruit soup cockaigne, orange fruit soup - strawberries Romanoff, blueberries or huckleberries, cranberry sauce or jelly, spiced cranberry jelly) creased and crumpled along page margin. Pages 190 - 191 (tuna, noodle and mushroom soup casserole, lasagne, canneloni or manicotti, ravioli, ravioli filling, cheese dumplings, quick cheese dumplings); page 440 (braised liver with

vegetables, braised liver cockaigne with wine, beef liver creole, liver with peppers and onions and olives on skewers); page 599 (strudel continued, about meringue paste); page 625 (marble cake, whipped cream cake, sour cream cake, gold layer cake); pages 634 - 635 (chiffon oil cake, chiffon mocha oil cake, quick white oil cake, quick spice oil cake, quick chocolate oil cake, hurry-up cake, hurry-up caramel cake, hurry-up cocoa cake, hurry-up spice cake,

caramel cornflake ring); 370 - 371 (Florentines, leaf wafers, almond meringue rings, cinnamon stars, nut and date cookies, macaroons, tea wafers); 677 - 679 (maple sugar icing, chocolate marshmallow icing, chocolate-fudge icing, brown sugar marshmallow icing, quick white icing, royal glaze or Swiss meringue or quick decorative icing, lemon topping for cookies or bars, quick lemon icing, three-minute icing, French icing, cream cheese icing, quick orange icing, butterscotch icing, chocolate butter icing, quick brown sugar icing, chocolate cream cheese icing, European chocolate icing, easy chocolate icing, quick chocolate icing, coffee or mocha icing, quick maple icing, quick honey peanut-butter icing) stained and caked with food. There is a dried piece of onion between the pages. Pages 211 - 214 (about pancakes griddle or batter cakes, whole-grain griddle cakes, graham griddle cakes, French pancakes, stuffed French pancakes or crêpes, gateau crêpe, fruit pancakes, blintzes or cottage cheese pancakes, crêpes Suzettes, Henri's butter sauce for crêpes Suzettes, pfannkukchen or German pancakes, Austrian pancakes or mockerlin, Russian raised pancakes or blini, sour milk pancakes); 645 - 651 (sweetened whipped cream or crème chantilly fillings, custard cream pastry filling or crème patissière, frangipane cream, mocha filling, ricotta chocolate filling, lemon filling, lemon orange custard filling, chocolate fruit filling, apricot custard filling, orange cream filling, ginger fruit filling, almond or fig or raisin filling, toasted walnut or pecan filling, almond or hazelnut custard filling, high altitude angel cake, high altitude chocolate angel cake, high altitude spice angel cake, high altitude white cake, high altitude fudge cake, high altitude two-egg cake, high altitude cocoa cake, high altitude sponge cake, high altitude gingerbread,

lemon filling, lemon orange custard filling, chocolate fruit filling, apricot custard filling, orange cream filling, ginger fruit filling, almond or fig or raisin filling, toasted walnut or pecan filling, almond or hazelnut custard filling, high altitude angel cake, high altitude chocolate angel cake, high altitude spice angel cake, high altitude white cake, high altitude fudge cake, high altitude two-egg cake, high altitude cocoa cake, high altitude sponge cake, high altitude gingerbread,

brownies cockaigne, butterscotch brownies, molasses bars, Christmas chocolate bars cockaigne, German honey bars, date or fig or prune bars, about cake houses, about drop cookies, tortelettes, butterless drop cookies, drop butter wafers, chocolate-chip drop cookies, sugar drop cookies with oil, ginger thins, anise drop cookies, rocks or fruit drop cookies, hermits, pfeffernüsse, German honey cookies, carrot drop cookies, quick oatmeal cookies, oatmeal gems)

Christmas cookies) buckled and stained. Pages 604 - 608 (mock mince pie, prune or apricot pie, raisin pie, linzertorte, banbury tarts, crumb or gravel pie, Jefferson Davis pie, chess tarts, pecan pie, transparent pie, pumpkin or squash pie, apple or peach or plum cake cockaigne, skillet or upside-down cake, fresh fruit crisp or paradise, quick cherry crunch, sweet turnovers or rissoles, fruit dumplings, raised dumplings or dampfnudeln); 652 - 657 (about squares and bars,

buckled and stained and caked with food. Pages 293 - 294 (stuffed potato cups, tiny new potatoes sautéed, lyonnaise potatoes, franconia or browned potatoes, potatoes Anna, hashed brown potatoes, potato pancakes, grated potatoes, pan-broiled, soufflé or puffed potatoes); 609 - 613 (custard or cream pie, custard tarts or flan with fruit, chocolate-topped custard pie, caramel custard pie, chocolate pie, chocolate cream pie,

coffee tarts or pie, butter-scotch pie, orange cream pie, bakers' cheese pie or cake, whipped cream cheesecake, sour cream cheesecake, gelatin cheese cake, fruit gelatin cheesecake, ricotta cheese pie or cake); 639 - 641 (chocolate walnut torte, chocolate date torte, poppy seed custard torte, sachertorte, génoise, trifle or rasberry rum cake, orange-filled cake, Boston cream pie or cake, cream meringue tart cockaigne); 658 -661 (glazed or flourless

oatmeal wafers, orange-marmalade drops, peanut-butter cookies, butterscotch nut cookies, coconut meringue cookies, coconut macaroons, chocolate co-conut macaroons, cocoa kisses, chocolate cracker kisses, vanilla refrigerator cookies, butterscotch refrig-erator cookies, chocolate refrigerator cookies, pin-wheel refrigerator cookies, molasses crisps cockaigne, refrigerator lace cookies, jubilee wafers, roll cookies, rich roll cookies, butter thins); 664 - 669 (chocolate

almond shells, speculatius, cookie-press or spritz cookies, about filled cookies and filled bars, jelly tots, macaroon jam tarts, individual nut tarts, pecan or angel slices, plum bombs, Frankfurter oblaten, butter krumkakes, lemon krum-kakes, ice cream cones or gaufrettes, almond curls or fortune cookies, brandy snaps, maple curls, curled caramel cookies, curled nut wafers, pecan drop cookies, nut wafers, pecan or benne wafers, molasses nut wafers, hazelnut wafers,

flourless nut balls, pecan puffs); 676 (chocolate coating over boiled white icing, seven-minute white icing, seven-minute lemon icing, seven-minute orange icing, seven-minute sea-foam icing, fondant icing, luscious orange icing, caramel icing) stained. Pages 590 - 596 (flour paste pie crust, quick and easy pie crust, hot-water pie crust, wheatless pie crust, pâte brisée, rich egg pie crust or muerbeteig or pâte sucrée, Vienna pastry,

cheese-cake crust, graham cracker or zweiback or ginger snap crust, luxury crumb crust, cereal pie crust, cookie crumb crust, puff paste or pâte feuilletée); 601 - 602 (apple tarts, peach pie, berry pie with fresh fruit, fresh cherry pie, berry or cherry pie with cooked fruit, berry or cherry pie with frozen fruit, German cherry pie, sour cream cherry pie, strawberry or raspberry pie, glazed fruit pie) stained with oil. Pages 627 - 628 (lady cake, chocolate cake, fudge layer cake, fudge meringue cake, devil's food cake cockaigne, old-world chocolate spice cake with citron, spiced chocolate spice cake with citron, spiced chocolate and prune cake, chocolate apricot cake, velvet spice cake) stained and torn in the middle. Pages 662 - 663 (sand tarts, ginger snaps, gingerbread men, almond pretzels or mandelplaettchen, Scotch shortbread, yolk cookies, springerle) stained and caked with food. Loose stained pages 405 - 406

from unidentified cookbook showing glossary of fish names from red salmon to shortbill spearfish holding place between pages 358 - 359 (casseroled octopus, broiled salt mackerel, broiled fresh mackerel, broiled salt mackerel, pompano en papillote, broiled salmon steaks or darnes, cold glazed salmon, about roe and milt). Ribbon marking place between pages 700 - 701 (pearl-tapioca pudding, bread pudding with meringue, brown Betty, prune or apricot Betty, baked pineapple Betty, baked fig pudding, baked date ring or Christmas wreath, baked plum pudding, cottage pudding) and pages 728 - 729 (soft center fondant, uncooked fondant, caramel fondant, Newport creams or centers, opera creams or centers, maple cream candy, peppermint cream wafers, almond or filbert paste, marzipan or marchpane). Other minor stains passim not recorded. Gen. friable and dilapidated.

Joy of Cooking

Irma S. Rombauer, Marion Rombauer Becker and Ethan Becker. Hardback with dust jacket. One Integral ribbon. Great Britain. Simon & Schuster UK Ltd. 1999. ISBN 0 684 85146 6. Good condition. Ribbon marking place between pages 166 -167 (barbecued kebabs, affettato, Tuscan dipping sauce for raw vegetables, melon and figs wrapped in prosciutto, fennel wrapped in prosciutto, bocconcini, white bean and roast garlic purée, bruschetta with tomatoes and basil). Page from a Sunday supplement (Chubby Charms: Gnocchi Like Mama Makes by Annie Bell) marking place between pages 106 - 107 (Spanish garlic soup with eggs, chicken noodle soup, chicken rice or barley soup, chicken soup with ravioli or tortellini, matzo ball soup, chicken or beef consommé, consommé brunoise, miso).

Note
The term dog eared has
been applied to all
corners which have been
turned down, whether this
turning down was
deliberate or not. Sharp
creases have been
recorded
separately.

Index

-A-

A Book of Middle Eastern Food, Claudia Roden 35

A bowl of fresh herbs 34

A good whole-wheat bread 31

A lady, editor of The Jewish Manual, introduction by Chaim Raphael

A Nun's Sigh 21

A Taste of the West Country in Food and in Pictures, Theodora Fitzgibbon 16

About accessory factors 37

About buffet service continued 38

About cake houses 40

About drop cookies

About filled cookies and filled bars 41

About meringue paste 38

About pancakes or griddle or batter cakes 39

About roe and milt 42

About squares and bars 40

Abulon en escabeche 33

Affettato 43

Agrodolce alla trapanese, tonno in 3

Aïoli 34

Albemarle peach chutney 21

Albert biscuits 37

Alla bolognese, tagliatelle 9

Alla ghiotta, paglia e fieno

All'Alfredo, fettuccine

Almond blancmange 17

Almond cookies 40

Almond cookies, Chinese 30

Almond chocolate shells 41

Almond curls or fortune cookies

Almond meringue rings 39

Almond or fig or raisin filling 39

Almond or filbert paste 43

Almond or hazelnut custard filling 39

Almond pretzels 30

Almond pretzels or mandel-plaettchen 42

Almonds salted 8

Amaretto soufflé 24

Amberjack 7

Ambrosia 21

American Cooking, Dale Brown and the editors of Time-Life Books 23

American Cooking, hard board folder

American Cooking: The Melting Pot, James P. Shenton, Angelo M. Pellegrini, Dale Brown, Israel Shenker, Peter Wood and the editors of Time-Life Books 24

An egg hors d'ouevre 35

An Invitation to Indian Cooking, Madhur Jaffrey 20

An Omelette and a Glass of Wine, Elizabeth David 12

An open wood fire 14

Anadama bread 31

Anchovies, cold spaghetti salad with olives and ... 3

Anchovy sandwich 31

Angel cake, high altitude 39

Angel chocolate cake, high altitutde

Angel or pecan slices 41

Angel spice cake, high altitude 39

Anise caps 30

Anise drop cookies 40

Anna, pommes 28

Anna, potatoes 40

Another identical 33

Äoli 34

Aoyagi, Akiko and William Shurtleff, The Book of Tofu: Food for Mankind 15

Appareil à bombe 29

Apple brown Betty 30, 42

Apple brown Betty, down East 21

Apple Charlotte 30

Apple double cake or cup-cakes

Apple dumplings

Apple, fresh cookies

Apple or peach or plum cake cockaigne   40

Apple or prune or apricot or pineapple sauce cookies   30

Apple pan dowdy   21, 30

Apple pie   21

Apple, raw cake or bread   30

Apple sauce   21

Apple sauce cake   30

Apple slump, Louisa May Alcott's   21

Apple soufflé with lemon-nutmeg sauce   17

Apple tarts   42

Apples, crab   21

Apples in dressing gowns   37

Apples, sheet cake filled with   10

Apples, slices with choco-late   37

Apricot chocolate cake   42

Apricot custard filling   39

Apricot or prune Betty   42

Apricot prune or apple or pineapple sauce cookies   30

Apricot prune pie   40

Apricot pineapple conserve   31

Apricot pudding   36

Armenian meat soup with burghul

Aromatic oil   5

Arroz a la Mexicana   33

Artichoke hearts and broad beans in oil   36

Artichoke hearts stewed in oil   35

Artichokes, jerusalem pickled   21

Artichokes, stuffed baked   37

Asparagus, how to buy and prepare   11

Assorted fruit   38

Ataïf with cheese   35

Aubergine gratin from Provence   11

Aubergine purée   35

Aubergine purée with yoghourt

Aubergine slices stuffed with cream cheese

Aubergine sweet-sour Spanish style   11

Aubergines, fried with yoghourt   35

Aubergines, tomatoes and green peppers in oil continued   36

Austrian pancakes or nockerlin   39

Avocado purée carmel   35

Avocado purée with cream cheese

Avocado purée with tuna

Avocados, cheese and rice   17

Aztec Pie   33

-B-

Baba ghanoush   35

Babka made with pumpkin   37

Badly stained   8, 30

Baingan Bhurta continued   4

Baingan Bhurta Seekhi

Baked date ring or Christmas wreath   42

Baked fig pudding

Baked pineapple Betty

Baked plum pudding

Baked pumpkin, American   11

bakers' cheese pie or cake   41

Baking powder biscuits   23, 31

Ball, meat   36

Balls, rum or bourbon or sherry or brandy or walnut spirit   30

Banana fritters   18

Bananas flambées   21

Bananas, Octave Uzanne's   18

Banbury tarts   40

Bandhgobi parcha   4

Bandhgobi   turrcarri

Barbecued kebabs   43

Barbecued spare ribs   5

Barley soup or chicken rice   43

Bars and cookies, filled, about   41

Bars and squares, about 40

Bars, chocolate Christmas

Bars, date or fig or prune

Bars, German honey

Bars, molasses

Basic griddle cakes 31

Basic tomato sauce 32

Basil and tomatoes with bruschetta 43

Basque pepper and egg tarts 11

Batarkeh 35

Bateman, Michael, Caroline Conran, Oliver Gillie, The Sunday Times Guide to the World's Best Food 25

Bavarian cream, hazelnut 21

Bavarois à l'orange 9

Bavarois au chocolat

Bean, white and roast garlic purée 43

Beans, white, browned-in-the-oven 27

Beard, James, James Beard's American Cookery 30

Bêche-de-mer gourmet 7

Beck, Simone, Simca's Cuisine 4

Beck, Simone, Julia Child, Mastering the Art of French Cooking, Volume Two 28

Beck, Simone, Louisette Bertholle, Julia Child,

Mastering the Art of French Cooking, Volume I 9

Becker, Ethan, Marion Rombauer Becker, Irma S. Rombauer, Joy of Cooking 43

Becker, Marion Rombauer and Irma S. Rombauer, Joy of Cooking 37

Becker, Marion Rombauer, Irma S. Rombauer and Ethan Becker, Joy of Cooking 43

Beef and puréed vegetable soup 35

Beef, fillet of, with marchand de vin sauce

Beef liver creole 38

Beef or chicken consommé 43

Beer, pocket guide to 10

Beetroot stock 11

Behrens, Elsa, Cooking the Spanish Way 32

Beid bi gebna maqlia 36

Beid bi lamoun 35, 36

Beid bi tamatem 36

Beid bi tom

Beid hamine

Beid masluq

Beid masus

Beid mutajjan

Bell, Annie 43

Benne wafers or pecan 41

Bent 34

Berry grunt, Cape Cod 21

Berry or cherry pie with frozen fruit 42

Berry pie with fresh fruit

Bertholle, Louisette, Julia Child, Simone Beck, Mastering the Art of French Cooking, Volume I 9

Betty, apple brown 30, 42

Betty, apple brown down East 21

Betty, apricot or prune 42

Betty, baked pineapple

Bhurta taingan continued 4

Bhurta tamattar

Birthday card from Florence 11

Birthday card from Val and Geoffrey

Biscuits, Albert 37

Biscuits, baking powder 23, 31

Biscuits, buttermilk

Blackcurrent sorbet 18

Blancmange 21

Blancmange, almond 17

Blancmange, coconut

Blancmange, old-fashioned 30

Blank slip 48

Blehat samak 35, 36

Blini or Russian raised pancakes 39

Blintzes or cottage cheese pancakes 39

Blotch, small 22

Blotched   22

Blue fish   7

Blueberries or huckleberries   38

Blueberry grunt   30

Blueberry shortcake   21

Blumenthal, Heston   18

Bocconcini   43

Boiled or poached fish   36

Boiled white icing over chocolate coating   41

Bolognese sauce   9

Bombe glacée à l'abricot

Bombes, Ice Cream, Sorbets, Frozen Yogourts, Parfaits, Bombes and More, Shona Crawford Poole   18

Bombs, plum   41

Bookmark   7, 10, 11, 15, 18, 28, 33

Borshch, Russian continued   11

Borshch, simplified variations

Boston cream pie or cake   41

Bouillabaisse   38

Bourbon or sherry or rum or brandy balls or walnut spirit balls   30

Brabant purée   10

Brain salad   35

Braised liver cockaigne with wine   38

Braised liver with vegetables

Bran muffins   31

Brandy or bourbon or sherry or rum or walnut spirit balls   30

Brandy, grape   32

Brandy snaps   41

Bread, a good whole-wheat   31

Bread, Anadama

Bread and butter pudding, The Coach House   30

Bread, brown   31

Bread, corn... (Jeanne Owen's)

Bread, French   38

Bread, health   31

Bread, hot-water

Bread, Middle Eastern

Bread pudding with meringue   42

Bread, rye   31

Bread, Swedish limpa

Bread, whole-grain

Bream, Ray's   7

Breakfast menus   38

Bredie, meat   20

Broad beans and artichoke hearts in oil   36

Broiled fresh mackerel   42

Broiled grapefruit   31

Broiled salmon steaks or darnes   42

Broiled salt mackerel

Broken into two   35

Broken spine   8, 9 , 10, 13, 27, 30

Brown Betty, apple   30, 42

Brown Betty, down East apple   21

Brown bread   31

Brown, Dale and the editors of Time-Life Books, American Cooking   23

Brown, Dale, James P. Shenton, Angelo M. Pellegrini, Israel Shenker, Peter Wood and the editors of Time-Life Books, American Cooking: The Melting Pot   24

Brown sugar icing, quick   39

Brown sugar marshmallow icing

Brown sugar or tan or pecan kisses   30

Browned or franconia potatoes   37, 40

Browned-in-the-oven white beans   27

Brownies   30

Brownies, butterscotch   40

Brownies cockaigne

Bruschetta with tomatoes and basil   43

Brussel sprouts, gratin of continued   10

Brussel sprouts soup

Bstilla   35

Bublanina   26

Buckled, all pages   25

Buckled and stained   31

Buckled, marked and ... in a circular pattern   12

Buckled page 3, 26. 27, 30

Buckled pages 29, 31, 39, 40

Buckled two back pages 26

Buckwheat cakes   38

Budín de merluza con mayonesa   32

Burghul, Armenian meat soup with   36

Burned   12

Burritos   33

Burro e formaggio con polenta   9

Butter, fish fried in   36

Butter krumkakes   41

Butter, parsley with cauliflower   11

Butter sauce, Henri's for crêpes Suzettes   39

Butter thins   41

Butter wafers, drop   40

Buttered rum   38

Butterless drop cookies 40

Buttermilk biscuits   31

Buttermilk pancakes

Butters, fruit

Butterscotch brownies 40

Butterscotch icing   39

Butterscotch nut cookies 41

Butterscotch pie

Butterscotch refrigerator cookies

-C-

Cabbage, stuffed whole with sauerkraut

Cacao, sorbet au   24

Cake, apple sauce   30

Cake, caramel hurry-up 38

Cake, carrot, fresh   30

Cake, cherry, my Mother's 10

Cake, chiffon mocha oil 38

Cake, chiffon oil

Cake, chocolate   42

Cake, chocolate angel high altitude   39

Cake, chocolate apricot 42

Cake, chocolate custard or devil's food   30

Cake, chocolate or chocolate caramel potato

Cake, chocolate, spiced ... and prune   42

Cake, chocolate upside-down   30

Cake, double apple or cupcakes

Cake, cocoa hurry-up 38

Cake, coffee with crumble top   37

Cake, corn as in Transdanubia   10

Cake, crazy or crazy mixed-up   30

Cake, crumble   37

Cake, devil's food cockaigne

Cake, devil's food or chocolate custard   30

Cake Doughnuts   31

Cake, fudge   30

Cake, fudge layer   42

Cake, fudge meringue

Cake, gelatine cheese ... 41

Cake, gold layer   38

Cake, high altitude angel 39

Cake, high altitude cocoa

Cake, high altitude fudge

Cake, high altitude spice angel

Cake, high altitude sponge 39

Cake, high altitude two-egg 39

Cake houses, about 40

Cake, hurry-up   38

Cake, hurry-up caramel

Cake, hurry-up cocoa

Cake, hurry-up spice

Cake, lady   42

Cake, marble   17, 38

Cake, mayonnaise   30

Cake, Norwegian mocha 17

Cake, oil, quick chocolate 38

Cake, oil, quick spice

Cake, oil, quick white

Cake, old-world chocolate spice cake with citron 42

Cake, orange-filled 41

Cake or bread, raw apple 30

Cake or pie, bakers' cheese

Cake or pie, Boston cream

Cake or pie, ricotta cheese

Cake, pork

Cake, pumpkin or squash spice

Cake, raspberry rum or trifle 41

Cake, red devil's food 30

Cake, red velvet

Cake, sheet filled with apples 42

Cake, sour cream 38

Cake, spice hurry-up

Cake, spiced chocolate spice with citron 42

Cake, sweet chocolate 30

Cake, upside-down or skillet 40

Cake, velvet spice 42

Cake, whipped cream 38

Cake, whipped cream cheese 41

Cake, white high altitude 39

Cake, yeast coffee 37

Caked 3, 4, 11, 12, 21, 27, 29, 31, 32, 33, 34, 36, 39, 40, 42

Cakes, buckwheat 38

Cakes, fried rice 31

Cakes, potato and ham 38

Camarones escorpionados con chile rojo 33

Camarones, ensalada de

Canapés, Christmas 38

Canapés, tarts and tartlets for

Candied cranberries 21

Candy, cream 42

Cannelloni 38

Cape Cod berry grunt 21

Cappelletti di pesce col sugo di gamberetti continued 3

Caramel cake, hurry-up 38

Caramel cornflake ring 39

Caramel custard pie 40

Caramel fondant 43

Caramel icing 41

Caraway macaroni rabbit 17

Carciofi, lasagne coi 3

Carmel avocado purée

Carne, chili con 30

Carne o pesce tri i due piatti 3

Carrot cookies 30

Carrot drop cookies 40

Carrot, fresh, cake 30

Carrot pickles 21

Carrot salad, Gujerati 10

Casserole, sausage and macaroni 15

Casserole, tuna, noodle and mushroom soup 38

Casseroled octopus 42

Cauliflower and green bean salad 11

Cauliflower, Greek

Cauliflower in the Sicilian style

Cauliflower, red hot

Cauliflower soup, Michael Smith's

Cauliflower with parsley butter

Cavolfiore, penne col sugo di 3

Cereal pie crust 42

Chaah sieu 5

Chakchouka 36

Chamberlain, Lesley, The Food and Cooking of Russia 6

Champignons, petit salé aux

Charcuterie and French Pork Cookery, Jane Grigson 27

Charleston pudding 30

Charms, chubby 43

Chaussons 9

Cheese and rice avocados 17

Cheese, ataïf with 35

Cheese, cottage ... sandwich   31

Cheese, cream, aubergine slices stuffed with

Cheese dumplings

Cheese dumplings, quick   38

Cheese, grilled or fried   35

Cheese, ricotta pie or cake   41

Cheesecake crust   42

Cheesecake, gelatine

Cheesecake, gelatine fruit

Cheesecake, sour cream

Cheesecake, whipped cream

Cherry cake, my Mother's   10

Cherry crunch, quick   41

Cherry pie, fresh   42

Cherry pie, German

Cherry or berry pie with frozen fruit

Cherry pie with cooked fruit

Cherry pie with sour cream

Cherubs or honeymoon or dream bars or lover's morsels   30

Chess tarts   40

Chicken liver, fried eggs with   36

Chicken liver timbales   17

Chicken livers en brochette

Chicken livers Madeira

Chicken noodle soup   43

Chicken or beef consommé

Chicken rice or barley soup

Chicken soup with ravioli or tortellini

Chicken, tandori-style   10

Chiffon mocha oil cake   38

Chiffon oil cake

Child, Julia, Simone Beck, Louisette Bertholle, Mastering the Art of French Cooking, Volume I   9

Child, Julia, Simone Beck, Mastering the Art of French Cooking, Volume Two   28

Chile rojo con camarones escorpionados   33

Chile verde y papas, sopa di

Chili con carne   30

Chinese almond cookies

Chinese leaf, how to choose and prepare continued   11

Chinese leaf, stir-fried

Chinese Food, Kenneth Lo   5

Chinese Regional Cookery, Margaret Leeming and May Huang Man-hui   14

Chocolat praliné, glace au   29

Chocolat, Bavarois au   9

Chocolate almond shells   41

Chocolate angel cake, high altitude   39

Chocolate apricot cake   42

Chocolate butter icing   39

Chocolate cake   42

Chocolate cake or chocolate caramel potato cake   30

Chocolate caramel potato cake or chocolate cake

Chocolate Christmas bars cockaigne   40

Chocolate coating over boiled white icing   41

Chocolate coconut macaroons

Chocolate cracker kisses

Chocolate cream cheese icing   39

Chocolate cream pie   40

Chocolate custard or devil's food cake   30

Chocolate date torte   41

Chocolate fruit filling   39

Chocolate icing, easy

Chocolate icing, European

Chocolate icing, quick

Chocolate marshmallow icing

Chocolate oil cake, quick   38

Chocolate pie   40

Chocolate pite, latticed   10

Chocolate refrigerator cookies 41

Chocolate ricotta filling 39

Chocolate roll continued 30

Chocolate sauce, lobster with 24

Chocolate slices 37

Chocolate slices with apples

Chocolate soufflé 17, 30

Chocolate spice cake, old-world with citron 42

Chocolate, spiced ... and prune cake

Chocolate spiced spice cake with citron

Chocolate sweet cake 30

Chocolate, sweet or chocolate chunk or chocolate chip or Toll House cookies

Chocolate upside-down cake

Chocolate walnut torte 41

Chocolate-chip drop cookies 40

Chocolate-fudge icing 39

Chocolate-topped custard pie 40

Chorros, frijoles 33

Chou farci 28

Chou feuilles de

Choux pastry for cream buns or éclairs 37

Choux, petit salé au 27

Christmas canapés 38

Christmas chocolate cockaigne 40

Christmas cookies 39

Christmas wreath or baked date ring 42

Chubby charms 43

Chutneys and pickles 22

Cinnamon stars 39

Circular pattern 12

Citron, old-world chocolate spice cake with 42

Citron, spiced chocolate spice cake with

Clafouti aux prunes 29

Claiborne, Craig and Virginia Lee, The Chinese Cookbook 17

Claiborne, Craig, The New York Times Cookbook

Clover leaf rolls 23

Cobbler, peach 21

Cocoa cake, high altitude 39

Cocoa cake, hurry-up 38

Cocoa kisses 41

Cocktails, sausages with 30

Coconut blancmange 17

Coconut chocolate macaroons 41

Coconut macaroons

Coconut meringue cookies

Coconut pudding 17

Coctel de abulon 33

Coctel de mariscos

Coda alla vaccinara 7

Coetzee, Renata, The South African Culinary Tradition with 167 Authentic Recipes 25

Coeur à la Crème 32

Coffee cake, yeast 37

Coffee cake with crumble top

Coffee or mocha icing 39

Coffee tarts or pie 41

Cold cucumber and yoghourt soup 35

Cold glazed salmon 42

Cold mussel plaki 35

Cold spaghetti salad with anchovies and olives 3

Cold stuffed vine leaves 35

Cold-water bread 31

Colle, Marie-Pierre and Guadalupe Rivera, Frida's Fiestas: Recipes and Reminiscences of Life with Frida Kahlo. Translator (text), Kenneth Krabbenhoft, translator (recipes), Olga Rigsby 7

Colonial cheese pudding 31

Coming away 17, 37

Conran, Caroline, editor and adaptor, Cuisine Gourmande by Michel Guérard 17

Conran, Caroline, Michael Bateman, Oliver Gillie, The Sunday Times Guide to the World's Best Food   25

Conserve, apricot pineapple   31

Consommé beef or chicken   43

Consommé brunoise

Cooked fruit, cherry pie with   42

Cookie crumb crust   41

Cookie-press or spritz cookies

Cookies and bars, filled, about 41

Cookies, almond   30

Cookies, almond (or fortune)

Cookies, anise drop   40

Cookies, apple or prune or apricot or pineapple sauce   30

Cookies, butterscotch nut   41

Cookies, butterscotch refrigerator

Cookies, caramel curled

Cookies, carrot   30

Cookies, carrot drop   40

Cookies, Chinese almond   30

Cookies, chocolate refrigerator   41

Cookies, chocolate-chip drop   40

Cookies, Christmas   39

Cookies, coconut meringue   41

Cookies, cookie-press (or spritz)

Cookies, date and nut   38

Cookies, drop about   40

Cookies, drop butterless

Cookies, fresh apple   30

Cookies, fruit drops (or rocks)   40

Cookies, honey German

Cookies, mincemeat   30

Cookies, molasses

Cookies, oatmeal quick

Orange-marmalade drops   41

Cookies, peanut-butter

Cookies, pecan drop   40

Cookies, pinwheel refrigerator   41

Cookies, refrigerator lace

Cookies, roll

Cookies, rich roll

Cookies, rolled   30

Cookies, stick candy

Cookies, sugar drop with oil   40

Cookies, sweet chocolate or chocolate chunk or chocolate chip or Toll House   30

Cookies, vanilla refrigerator   41

Cookies, yolk   42

Cooking the Greek Way, Maro Duncan   12

Cooking the Hungarian Way, Kato Frank   9

Cooking the Polish Way, Lila Kowalska   37

Cooking the Spanish Way, Elsa Behrens   32

Cooking with Pomiane, Edouard de Pomiane   13

Corn Cake as in Transdanubia   10

Corn flapjacks, crisp   38

Cornmeal pancakes

Cornmeal griddle cakes

Corn tortillas, stone ground   33

Cornbread, Jeanne Owen's   31

Cornflake caramel ring   39

Cornmeal muffins   31

Costa, Margaret, Recipes: The Cooking of Italy 24

Côtes de Porc à la bayonnaise   28

Côtes de porc à la charcutiere

Côtes de porc au vin blanc

Côtes de porc sautées à la gasconne

Cottage cheese pancakes or blintzes   39

Cottage cheese sandwich   31

Cottage pudding   42

Coupelles   29

Courgettes aux riz, tian de

Courgettes en persillade gratinées   28

Courgettes en pistouille

Courgettes etuvées à la crème continued

Courgettes farcies au riz et aux poivrons   29

Courgettes farcies aux amandes

Courgettes gratinées mornay   28

Courgettes rapées   29

Courgettes rapées sautées 29, 30

Courgettes tarts   13

Courgettes timbale de 29

Cousbareia sauce with fried fish   36

Cover(s)   passim

Crab apples, spiced 21

Crab meat salad, tomatoes stuffed with   37

Crab meat or lobster or shrimp sandwiches   31

Crab, quick-fried in aromatic oil   5

Cracked spine   6, 32

Cranberries, candied 21

Cranberry jelly, spiced 38

Cranberry sauce   21

Cranberry sauce or jelly 38

Crazy cake or crazy mixed-up cake   30

Cream and strawberries 32

Cream buns or éclairs, choux pastry for   37

Cream cheese

Cream cheese, aubergine slices stuffed with   35

Cream cheese, avocado purée with

Cream cheese, frangipane   39

Cream cheese icing

Cream, maple candy 43

Cream, meringue tart cockaigne   41

Cream, orange ... filling 39

Cream, orange ... pie 41

Cream, peppermint ... wafers   43

Cream or custard pie 40

Creams or centers, Newport 42

Creams opera

Crease   25

Creased 21, 27, 34, 35, 38

Creases   43

Crème au beurre à la meringue Italienne

Crème Chantilly or sweetened whipped cream fillings   39

Crème patissière or custard cream pastry filling

Crêpe gateau

Crêpes or French pancakes, stuffed

Crêpes Suzettes

Crevice   11

Crisp corn flapjacks 38

Crisp, fresh fruit or paradise 40

Crisps, molasses cockaigne

Croquettes   9

Crossed-out   25, 33

Crullers   31

Crumb crust, luxury   41

Crumb or gravel pie 40

Crumble cake   37

Crumbs   3, 31

Crumpled   21, 34, 38

Crumpled, slightly   7

Crunch, cherry quick 40

Crust, cereal pie   42

Crust, cheesecake

Crust, cookie crumb

Crust, ginger snap or zwie-back or graham cracker

Crust, luxury crumb

Csirkeragu continued 4

Cucumber and youghourt soup   35

Cucumber sandwich 31

Cuisine Gourmande, Michel Guérard, edited and adapted by Caroline Conran   17

Cupcakes or cake, double apple   30

Curd doughs   4

Curd, lemon English   12

Curled caramel cookies   41

Curled nut wafers

Curling, top corners   32

Custard, apricot filling   39

Custard, chocolate or devil's food cake   30

Custard chocolate-topped … pie   40

Custard cream pastry filling or crème patissière   39

Custard filling, hazelnut or almond

Custard or cream pie   40

Custard orange lemon filling   39

Custard pie, caramel   40

Custard pie, chocolate

Custard poppy seed torte   41

Custard tarts or flan with fruit   40

Cut away   36

Cutting tools   8

Çalbir   36

-D-

Dainty sandwiches   31

Damaged corner   7

Damaged, slightly   22

Dampfnudeln or raised dumplings   40

Danish dishes, 88   3

Danish Cooking: A Penguin Handbook, Nika Standen Hazelton   18

Darnes or broiled salmon steaks   42

Date and nut cookies   38

Date chocolate torte   41

Date or fig or prune bars   40

Date ring, baked or Christmas wreath   42

David, Elizabeth, An Omelette and a Glass of Wine   12

David, Elizabeth, Spices, Salt and Aromatics in the English Kitchen   8

David, Elizabeth, English Bread and Yeast Cookery   19

David, Elizabeth, French Provincial Cooking   34

David, Elizabeth, Italian Food   28

David, Elizabeth, Summer Cooking   20

Davidson, Alan and Charlotte Knox, Seafood: A Connoisseur's Guide and Cookbook   34

Davidson, Alan, North Atlantic Seafood   19

Davidson, Alan, Mediterranean Seafood   7

Debris   11

Dedication 7, 11, 35

Dedichen, Hetna, 88 Danish Dishes   3

Deep-fried eggs   36

Deep-fried or grilled small fish

Detached   15, 28, 32, 37

Devil's food cake cockaigne   42

Devil's food cake, red   30

Devil's food or chocolate custard cake   30

Dharamjit Singh, Indian Cooking   4

Dilapidated   3, 6, 6, 15, 21, 27, 28. 32, 35, 36, 42

Dirty   23, 27

Disengaging from the body   35

Dog eared   9, 13

Dog eared, all pages   27

Dog eared at the bottom   38

Dog eared bottom corner   21

Dog eared covers   8, 27

Dog eared end pages   7

Dog eared front cover   5

Dog eared front pages

Dog eared page   30, 34, 37

Dog eared pages   28, 34, 36, 38

Dog eared title page   32

Dog eared top and bottom   37, 38

Dog eared whole   18

Dolphin Fish   7

Double apple cake or cup-cakes   30

Dough, basic   4

Doughs, curd

Doughnuts, cake   31

Doughnuts, raised

Dow See Loong Haah   5

Down East apple brown Betty   21

Dream bars or cherubs or honeymoon bars or lover's morsels   30

Dressing gowns, apples in

Dried   39

Drop butter wafers   40

Duck with tomato   10

Düğvün Çorbasi   36

Dukkah   35

Dumplings, apple   30

Dumplings, cheese   38

Dumplings, fruit   40

Dumplings, huckleberry   30

Dumplings, quick cheese

Dumplings, raised (or damp-fnudeln)   40

Duncan, Maro, Cooking the Greek Way   12

Dust jacket   3, 7, 10, 12, 13, 15, 19, 20, 22, 25, 34, 43

-E-

Easy chocolate icing   39

Éclairs or cream buns, choux pastry for   37

Edible wild plants   16

Editors of China Pictorial, Secrets of the Master Chefs of China   21

Editors of Time-Life Books and Dale Brown, American Cooking

Editors of Time-Life Books, and Helen and George Papashvily, The Cooking of Russia   26

Editors of Time-Life Books, and Israel Shenker, Dale Brown, James P. Shenton, Angelo M. Pellegrini, Peter Wood, American Cooking: The Melting Pot   24

Editors of Time-Life Books, and Joseph Wechsberg, The Cooking of Vienna's Empire   26

Editors of Time-Life Books, and Santha Rama Rau, The Cooking of India   22

Editors of Time-Life Books and Waverly Root, The Cooking of Italy   24

Egg and pepper tarts, Basque   11

Egg hors d'oeuvre   35

Egg sandwich   31

Eggah bi betingan   36

Eggah bi eish wa kousa

Eggah bi ferakh wa rishta

Eggah bi ful akhdar

Eggah bi korrat

Eggah bi kousa

Eggah bi lahma

Eggah bi mokh

Eggah bi sabaneh

Eggplant, stuffed with cheese   15

Eggs, deep-fried   36

Eggs fried with chicken liver

Eggs, hard-boiled

Eggs with potato and ham cakes   38

Eggs with Spanish garlic soup   43

Eggs, Scotch   30

Eggs, scrambled with vinegar   36

Elastic band   4, 5, 14, 27, 28, 32, 35

Electric ice cream machines   16

Elizabeth Borton de Treviño's best pudding

Elliot, Rose, The Bean Book   6

Ends, odds and   7

English Bread and Yeast Cookery, Elizabeth David   19

English Food, Jane Grigson   7

English Lemon curd   12

Ensalada de camarones   33

Ensalada de pescado

Ensalada de queso asadero

Escribe

Eshkeneh Shirazi   35

Espada (pesce) al salmoriglio   3

European chocolate icing   39

-F-

Facsimile   13

Fagioli dall'occhio con salsicce   9

Fair condition   23

Falafel or ta'amia   35

Fastnachts   21

Fata   36

Feng, Doreen Yen Hung, The Joy of Chinese Cooking   5

Fennel wrapped in prosciutto   43

Festival of the moon   5

Fettuccine all'Alfredo   9

Fettuccine con le zucchine frite   3

Feuilles de chou farcie   29

Fig or almond or raisin filling   39

Fig or date or prune bars   40

Fig pudding, baked   42

Figs and melon wrapped in prosciutto   43

Figs with prosciutto   31

Figs, roast (Mrs Crowen's)

Filbert or almond paste   43

Filled cookies and bars, about   41

Fillet of beef with marchand de vin sauce   37

Filling chocolate fruit   39

Filling, almond or hazelnut custard

Filling, apricot custard

Filling, custard cream pastry (or crème patissière)

Filling, ginger fruit

Filling, lemon

Filling, lemon or prune   40

Filling, mocha   39

Filling, orange cream

Filling, orange lemon custard

Filling, raisin or fig or almond   39

Filling, ravioli   38

Filling, ricotta chocolate   39

Filling, toasted walnut or pecan

Fillings, sweetened whipped cream (or crème Chantilly)

Fire, and open wood   14

Fish and meat sauces   25

Fish baked in the oven   36

Fish, boiled or poached

Fish, blue   7

Fish, dolphin

Fish fried in butter   36

Fish with cousbareia sauce

Fish in olive oil

Fish, kindred   7

Fish, names, glossary of   28, 42

Fish, pilot   7

Fish plaki   36

Fish, sciaenid   7

Fish, small, grilled or deep-fried   36

Fish, tuna... sandwich   31

Fitzgibbon, Theodora, A Taste of the West Country in Food and in Pictures   16

Flan   7

Flan aux prunes   29

Flan, Jane Grigson's kipper   13

Flan with fruit or custard tarts   40

Flapjacks, crisp corn   38

Flavoured grapefruit sections   31

Florentines   39

Flour paste pie crust   41

Flourless nut balls

Flourless or glazed oatmeal wafers

Flyleaf inscription   10, 11, 19, 33, 34

Flyleaf slight soiling

Flyleaf stained   3

Flyleaf stained and caked   12

Folded bottom corner   31

Folded plastic bag   33

Folded transparent food-bag 11

Fondant, caramel 43

Fondant icing 41

Fondant, soft center 42

Fondant, uncooked

Food for Free: A Guide to the Edible Wild Plants of Britain, Richard Mabey 16

Food processors 8

Food-bag 11

Fool, gooseberry 31

Formaggio e burro con polenta 9

Fortune cookies or almond curls 41

Fragment 32

Fraises ou framboises glacée, mousse aux 29

Framboises glacée ou fraises, mousse aux

Franconia or browned potatoes 37, 40

Frangipane cream 39, 40

Frank, Kato, Cooking the Hungarian Way 9

Frankfurter oblaten 41

Frayed covers 7

Frayed spine 4, 5, 27

Free 16

French bread 38

French dressing with mixed salad greens

French icing 39

French pancakes

French pancakes or crêpes, stuffed

French Provincial Cooking, Elizabeth David 34

French Provincial Cooking, loose page from 28

Fresh apple cookies 30

Fresh carrot cake

Fresh cherry pie 41

Fresh fruit crisp or paradise 40

Fresh fruit, berry pie with 41

Fresh herbs, a bowl of 35

Friable 7, 15, 21, 27, 28, 32, 35, 36, 43

Frida's Fiestas: Recipes and Reminiscences of Life with Frida Kahlo, Guadalupe Rivera and Marie-Pierre Colle, Kenneth Krabbenhoft (translator text), Olga Rigsby (translator recipes) 7

Fried aubergines with yoghourt 35

Fried Eggs with chicken liver 36

Fried fish with cousbareia sauce

Fried liver pieces 35

Fried or Grilled Cheese

Fried rice cakes 31

Frijoles, chorros 33

Fritters, banana 18

Fritters, cornmeal and oxtail with prunes

Fritters, fruit 21

Frosted grapes 31

Frozen fruit, berry or cherry pie with 41

Frozen plum pudding 21

Frozen uncooked ... jams 31

Fruit, assorted 38

Fruit, berry pie with fresh 41

Fruit butters 31

Fruit, crisp fresh or paradise 40

Fruit drop cookies or rocks

Fruit dumplings

Fruit fritters 21

Fruit gelatine cheesecake 41

Fruit, ginger ... filling 39

Fruit pancakes

Fruit pie, glazed 41

Fruit soup cockaigne 38

Fruit soup, orange

Fruit with flan or custard tarts 40

Fruits, salpiçon of 21

Fudge cake 30

Fudge cake, high altitude 39

Fudge layer cake 42

Fudge meringue cake

Ful nabed soup, 35

-G-

Gallette de pommes de terre farcie 28

Gallette de pommes de terre au fromage

Gamberetti, sugo di ... col cappellettti di pesce 3

Gamberi dorati

Gamberi, umido di ... col pomodoro piccante

Garlic, roast purée and white bean 43

Garlic, soup Spanish with eggs

Gateau aux noix 29

Gateau crêpe 39

Gaufrettes or ice cream cones 41

Gebna beida 35

Gelatine cheesecake 41

Gelatine fruit cheesecake

Gelato chef 18

Gems, oatmeal 40

Génoise

Genoise electrique 29

German cherry pie 41

German honey bars 40

German honey cookies

German pancakes or pfannkukchen 39

Gift, given as 27

Gillie, Oliver, Caroline Conran, Michael Bateman, The Sunday Times Guide to the World's Best Food 25

Ging Jeung Ngaap 5

Ginger and orange water ice 18

Ginger fruit filling 39

Ginger pears 21

Ginger snap or zwieback or graham cracker crust 42

Ginger thins 40

Gingerbread 31

Gingerbread men 30, 42

Gingerbread, high altitude 39

Gingersnaps 30

Glace au chocolat pralinée: le Kilimanjaro continued 29

Glace, Le Saint-Cyr

Glazed fruit pie 41

Glazed or flourless oatmeal wafers

Glossary of fish names

Glossy leaflet 33

Gnocchi like Mama makes 43

Gold layer cake 38

Golden buck 17

Good condition 13, 21, 22, 43

Good, otherwise in ... condition 34

Good Things, Jane Grigson 32

Good whole-wheat bread 31

Gooseberry fool

Gorgonzola col polenta 9

Gougère 17

Gourmet, Yuan Mei, her bêche-de mer 7

Graham cracker, zwieback or ginger snap crust 42

Graham griddle cakes 39

Grape brandy 32

Grapefruit, broiled 31

Grapefruit sections, flavoured

Grapes, frosted

grapes with brown sugar and sour cream

Grated potatoes 40

Gratin de potiron d'Arpajon 29

Gratin of brussel sprouts continued 10

Gratin, aubergine 11

Gravel or crumb pie 40

Graves, Eleanor, Great Dinners from Life 25

Gray, Rose and Ruth Rogers, River Café Cook Book Easy 10

Great Dinners from Life, Eleanor Graves 25

Greek cauliflower 11

Green bean and cauliflower salad

Green, Emily 20

Greens, salad 38

Greens, winter and spring

Grenadine Rothschild 17

Griddle cakes, basic 31

Griddle cakes, graham
39

Griddle cakes, onion
38

Griddle cakes, rice corn-
meal

Griddle cakes, rice flour

Griddle or batter or pan-
cakes, about   39

Griddlecakes, oatmeal
38

Griddle-cakes, whole-grain
39

Grigson, Jane, Charcuterie
and French Pork Cookery
27

Grigson, Jane, English Food
7

Grigson, Jane, Good Things
32

Grigson, Jane, Jane
Grigson's Fish book   28

Grigson, Jane, Jane
Grigson's Fruit Book   18

Grigson, Jane, Jane
Grigson's Vegetable Book
10

Grigson, Jane, The
Mushroom Feast   7

Grigson's, Jane, Kipper Flan
13

Grigson's, Jane, raised pie

Grill, mixed   14

Grilled or deep-fried small
fish   36

Grilled fried cheese   35

Grilled Trout   21

Grinder or hero or
submarine or sub sandwich
31

Ground-cherries poached

Grubby   24

Grunt   21, 30

Guérard, Michel, Cuisine
Gourmande, edited and
adapted by Caroline
Conran   17

Guide   37

Guide, beer   10

Guide, connoisseur's
34

Guide, definitive   18

Guide, The Sunday Times
25

Guide to edible wild plants
16

Gujerati carrot salad
10

Gurdakupura Turrcarri
4

-H-

Ham and potato cakes with
eggs   38

Hamud   35

Hard-boiled eggs   36

Haricot bean soup   35

Haroutunian, Arto der,
Vegetarian Dishes from the
Middle East   15

Haselnusstorte   26

Hashed brown potatoes
40

Havuç çorbasi   35

Hazan, Marcella, Marcella
Cucina   13

Hazan, Marcella, Marcella's
Italian Kitchen   12

Hazan, Marcella, The Classic
Italian Cookbook   8

Hazan, Marcella, The
Second Classic Italian Cookbook   3

Hazelnut Bavarian cream
21

Hazelnut or almond custard
filling   39

Hazelnut wafers

Hazelton, Nika Standen,
Danish Cooking: A Penguin
Handbook   18

Health bread   31

Heart   15

Hearts, artichoke and broad
beans in oil   36

Hearts, stewed in oil   35

Hearty pozole dinner
33

Henderson, Fergus, Nose to
Tail Eating: A Kind of British
Cooking   19

Henri Thiele's German pancakes   31

Henri's butter sauce for
crêpes Suzettes   39

Herb omelette   36

Herbs, fresh, a bowl of
35

Hermits   31, 40

Hero or grinder or submarine
or sub sandwich   31

High altitude angel cake
39

High altitude chocolate
angel cake

High altitude cocoa cake

High altitude fudge cake

High altitude gingerbread

High altitude spice angel cake

High altitude sponge cake

High altitude two-egg cake

High altitude white cake

Hippisley Coxe, Antony and Araminta, The book of the Sausage   32

Hole in page   29

Home on the Range: A Culinary History of the American West, Cathy Luchetti   34

Hominey, red ... stew from Jalisco   7

Honey, German ... bars 40

Honey, German ... cookies

Honey peanut-butter icing, quick   39

Honeydew melon, sliced rounds of filled with raspberries   38

Honeymoon bars or cherubs or dream bars or lover's morsels   30

Hoong sieu jüh yook 4

Hors d'oeuvre, egg 35

Hors d'oeuvres continued 9

Horse mackerel   7

Hot buttered rum   38

Hot sauce ravigote

Hot stuffed vine leaves 35

Hot-water bread   31

Hot-water pie crust   41

Houses, about cake

How to buy and prepare asparagus   11

How to choose and prepare Chinese leaf continued

Huang Man-hui, May and Margaret Leeming, Chinese Regional Cookery   14

Huckleberries or blueberries 38

Huckleberry dumplings 30

Hummus bi tahina   35

Hungarian Cooking, Fred Macnicol   4

Hünkâr beğendi   36

Hunting feasts, lampries in Ceylon   13

Hurry-up cake   38

Hurry-up caramel cake

Hurry-up cocoa cake

Hurry-up spice cake

-I-

Ice, ginger and orange water   18

Ice cream cones or gaufrettes   41

Ice cream makers, electric machines   16

Ice Cream, Sorbets, Frozen Yogourts, Parfaits, Bombes and More, Shona Crawford Poole   18

Ices: The Definitive Guide, Caroline Liddell and Robin Weir

Icing, chocolate marshmallow   39

Icing, brown sugar icing

Icing, Butterscotch

Icing, Caramel   41

Icing, chocolate butter 39

Icing, chocolate coating over boiled white

Icing, chocolate cream cheese

Icing, chocolate easy

Icing, marshmallow

Icing chocolate quick

Icing, chocolate-fudge

Icing, coffee or mocha

Icing, cream cheese

Icing, European chocolate

Icing, fondant

Icing, French

Icing, honey peanut-butter, quick

Icing, lemon seven-minute 41

Icing, luscious orange

Icing, maple sugar   39

Icing, mocha or coffee

Icing, quick brown sugar   39

Icing, quick decorative or royal glaze or Swiss meringue   39

Icing, quick honey peanut-butter

Icing, quick lemon

Icing, quick maple

Icing, quick orange

Icing, quick white

Icing, royal glaze or Swiss meringue or quick decorative

Icing, seven-minute orange 41

Icing, seven-minute sea-foam

Icing, seven-minute white

Icing, three-minute 39

Implements 29

In Search of Plenty: A History of Jewish Food, Oded Schwartz 8

Identical 33

Index 32, 38

Illustrations 29

Indian Cooking, Dharamjit Singh 4

Individual nut tarts 41

Information 13, 16

Inscription, flyleaf 10, 11, 19, 34

Inscription, flyleaf, pencilled 33

Inscription, inside board 25, 26

Inscription, title page 12

Inside and out 27

Inside, clipping 18

Inside cover 12, 35

Inside covers 10

Inside, information sheet 16

Inside inscription 25, 25

Inside, leaflet 18

Inside, sticker 25, 26

Inside, torn 37

Integral 34, 37, 43

Italian Food, Elizabeth David 28

-J-

Jackson, Michael, Pocket Beer Guide 10

Jaffrey, Madhur, An Invitation to Indian Cooking 20

Jaffrey, Madhur, Madhur Jaffrey's Indian Cookery

Jam macaroon tarts 41

Jam, strawberry, sun-cooked 21

James Beard's American Cookery, James Beard 30

Jams, uncooked frozen 31

Jane Grigson's Fish Book, Jane Grigson 28

Jane Grigson's Fruit Book, Jane Grigson 18

Jane Grigson's Vegetable Book, Jane Grigson 11

Japanese Cooking, Peter and Joan Martin 34

Jeanne Owen's cornbread 31

Jefferson Davis pie 40

Jelly tots 41

Jelly, cranberry (or sauce) 38

Jelly, orange 36

Jelly, spiced cranberry 38

Jerusalem artichokes, pickled 21

Joy of Cooking, Irma S. Rombauer and Marion Rombauer Becker 37

Joy of Cooking, Irma S. Rombauer, Marion Rombauer Becker and Ethan Becker. 43

Jubilee wafers 41

Jumbles 31

-K-

Kebabs, barbequed 43

Keh Jup Chow Haah Kow 5

Ketchup, tomato 21

Key lime pie 21

Khall wa-kardal 36

Kilimanjaro, le 29

Kindred fish 7

King Whitings 28

Kipper

Kipper, flan, Jane Grigson's 13

Kisses, chocolate cracker 41

Kisses, cocoa

Kisses, tan or brown sugar or pecan 30

Knox, Charlotte and Alan Davidson, Seafood: A Connoisseur's Guide and Cookbook 34

Koftit Ferakh

Kotopitta 35

Kousa bi gebna 36

Kowalska, Lila, Cooking the Polish Way 37

Krumkakes, butter 41

Krumkakes, lemon

Kuku sibzamini   36

Kukuye sabsi

-L-

La "Turta" di spinaci e riso 12

La bouillabaisse des pêcheurs continued 35

La bourride de Charles Bérot 34

La Charlotte Africaine 29

La Mexicana   33

Labaneya   35

Label, front cover   22

Ladoxitho   12

Lady cake   42

Lahma bi ajeen   35

Lamb, Welsh with laver 11

Lampries in Ceylon (hunting feasts) 13

Lang, George, The Cuisine of Hungary 10

Langue de chats   27

Langues de chats continued 29

Lard, petits pois au   27

Lard, pommes de terre au 28

Large Meat Pie   35

Lasagne   38

Lasagne coi carciofi   3

Latticed chocolate pite 10

Laver, Welsh lamb with 11

Le Kilimanjaro: Glace au chocolat pralinée continued 29

Le Saint-André, gateaux au noix

Le Saint-Cyr glace

Le Saint-Cyr glace continued

Leaf wafers   39

Leaf, Chinese, how to choose and prepare continued 11

Leaf, Chinese, stir-fried

Leberstreichwurst   32

Leberwurst

Lebkucken   30

Lee, Virginia and Craig Claiborne, The Chinese Cookbook 17

Leek pie   13

Leipoldt, C. Louis, Leipoldt's Cape Cookery 20

Leipoldt's Cape Cookery, C. Louis Leipoldt

Lemming, Margaret and May Huang Man-hui. Chinese Regional Cookery 14

Lemon curd, English 12

Lemon filling   39

Lemon icing, quick

Lemon icing, seven-minute 41

Lemon krumkakes

Lemon meringue pie 21

Lemon or prune filling 39

Lemon orange custard filling

Lemon soufflé   17

Lemon topping for cookies or bars

Lemon-nutmeg sauce, apple soufflé with

Lenguado a la crema 32

Lentil soup   35

Lentil and spinach soup

Leoni sausage   32

Lescó   10

Liddell, Caroline and Robin Weir, Ices: The Definitive Guide 18

Line, Yetty, Menus for Grills: Le Creuset   14

Linzertorte   40

Liptavsky syr   27

Liqueur, pineapple   32

Liver, beef ... creole 38

Liver, braised ... cockaigne with wine

Liver, braised with vegetables

Liver, chicken with fried eggs   36

Liver, pâté   38

Liver pieces, fried   35

Liver with peppers and onions and olives on skewers

Liver, chicken, timbales

Livers, chicken

Livers en brochette   17

Livers Madeira

Lo, Kenneth, Chinese Food 5

Loaves, sandwich   38

Lobster or shrimp or crab meat sandwiches   31

Lobster with a chocolate sauce   24

Loose, all pages after   32

Loose, beginning to work   38

Loose bundles of pages   5, 27

Loose, coming   38

Loose page   5, 13, 28, 34

Loose pages   4, 13, 34

Loose sections   13

Loose title page   27

Louisa May Alcott's apple slump   21

Lover's morsels or cherubs or honeymoon bars or dream bars   30

Luchetti, Cathy, Home on the Range: A Culinary History of the American West   34

Lunch box or picnic or tea sandwiches

Luscious orange icing   41

Luxury crumb crust

Lyonnaise potatoes   40

-M-

Mabey, Richard, Food for Free: A Guide to the Edible Wild Plants of Britain   16

Macaroni rabbit with caraway   17

Macaroni, casserole with sausage and   15

Macaroon jam tarts   41

Macaroons   38

Macaroons, chocolate coconut

Macaroons, coconut

Mackerel, broiled fresh   42

Mackerel, broiled salt

Mackerel, horse   7

Macnicol, Fred, Hungarian Cooking   4

Madhur Jaffrey's Indian Cookery, Madhur Jaffrey   10

Magimix mayonnaise   12

Making sauces in your Magimix food processor

Mama, gnocchi like ... makes   43

Mandelplaettchen or almond pretzels   42

Mankind   15

Manicotti   38

Maple cream candy   42

Maple curls   41

Maple icing quick   39

Maple sugar icing   30

Marble cake   17, 38

Marcella Cucina, Marcella Hazan   13

Marcella's Italian Kitchen, Marcella Hazan   12

Marchpane or marzipan   43

Margin, page   38

Marked   8

Marked and buckled   12

Marking, place   42, 43

Marinades and memories   20

Marshmallow brown sugar icing   39

Marshmallow chocolate icing

Martin, Peter and Joan, Japanese Cooking   34

Marzipan or marchpane   43

Mastering the Art of French Cooking, Volume Two, Julia Child and Simone Beck   28

Mastering the Art of French Cooking, Volume I, Simone Beck, Louisette Bertholle, Julia Child   9

Matzo ball soup   43

Mayonnaise cake   30

Mayonnaise, Magimix   12

Meagre   7

Meat and fish sauces   25

Meat ball soup   3

Meat bredie   20

Meat pie, large   35

Meat soup with burghul, Armenian   36

Mediterranean Seafood, Alan Davidson   7

Melanzane con spaghettini   8

Melanzane, parmagiana 11

Melokhia 35

Melon and figs wrapped in prosciutto 43

Melón escribe, sopa di 33

Men, gingerbread 30, 42

Menudo 33

Menus for Grills: Le Creuset, Yetty Line 14

Meringue almond ... rings 39

Meringue, coconut ... cookies 41

Meringue, cream ... tart cockaigne 41

Meringue, crème ou beurre à la

Meringue fudge cake 42

Meringue, lemon ... pie 21

Meringue paste, about 38

Meringue, Swiss or royal glaze or quick decorative icing 39

Meringue toppings 38

Meringue with bread pudding 42

Meringues, poires au sabayon 29

Merluza, budín de ... con mayonesa 32

Mexican Cooking at the Academy, Susan Lammers, editor, Vicki Barrios Schley and Angelo Villa, writers 33

Mexican rabbit 17

Mhaans turrcarri kahsta 4

Mhaans turrcarri sadah

Middle Eastern bread 31

Midye tavas 35

Milk, sour pancakes

Milt and row, about

Mince pie, mock 39

Mincemeat cookies 30

Minor (stains) 43

Mint condition 15, 19, 25

Mint, pepper 42

Miso 43

Missing, all pages after 27

Missing back cover 15, 21

Missing bibliographic data 15, 37

Missing covers 4, 6

Missing front corners 34

Missing front cover 5 32

Missing pages 15, 35

Missing spine 37

Mixed Grill 14

Mixed salad greens 38

Mixed-up, crazy 30

Mocha 17

Mocha chiffon oil cake

Mocha filling 39

Mocha or coffee icing

Mock mince pie

Molasses bars 40

Molasses cookies 30

Molasses crisps cockaigne 41

Molasses nut wafers

Moon, festival of 5

Morels, stuffed continued 10

Morue aux tomates 35

Morue en rayte

Mother's, cherry cake my ... 10

Moussaka 36

Mousse à l'Abricot Glacée 29

Mousse aux fraises ou aux framboises glacée 29

Mousse glacée pralinée aux noix (appareil à bombe)

Mrs Beeton neé Mayson, Mrs Beeton's Cookery Book 14

Mrs Beeton's Cookery Book, Mrs Beeton neé Mayson

Ms, in 21

Muerbeteig or pâte sucrée or pâte brisée 41

Muffins, bran 31

Muffins, cornmeal

Muffins, simple

Mulled wine or negus in quantity 38

Mullet, red small with garlic 36

Mushroom, tuna and noodle soup casserole 38

Mussel plaki, cold   35

My Mother's cherry cake   10

-N-

Nan, Roghni

Negus or mulled wine in quantity   38

New Indian Cooking, Meera Taneja   9

New Orleans Calas   21

Newport creams or centers   42

Newspaper clipping   15, 18, 20, 24

Nockerlin or Austrian pancakes   39

Noodle, chicken ... soup   43

Noodle, tuna and mushroom soup casserole   38

North Atlantic Seafood, Alan Davidson   19

Norwegian mocha cake   17

Not for sale in the U.S.A.   36

Nose to Tail Eating: A Kind of British Cooking, Fergus Henderson   19

Nut and date cookies   38

Nut balls, flourless   41

Nut butterscotch cookies

Nut molasses wafers

Nut tarts, individual

Nut wafers

Nut wafers, curled

-O-

Oatmeal cookies, quick

Oatmeal gems   40

Oatmeal griddle cakes   38

Oatmeal wafers, flourless or glazed   41

Octave Uzanne's bananas   18

Octopus, casseroled   42

Odds and ends   8

Oil, aromatic   5

Oil cake, chiffon

Oil cake, chiffon mocha

Oil cake, chocolate quick

Oil cake, quick spice

Oil cake, quick white

Oil cookies, sugar drop

Oil, olive   28, 26

Oil types   13

Ojja bi mergaz   36

Old-fashioned blancmange   30

Old-world chocolate spice cake with citron   42

Olive oil, fish in   36

Olive oil in cooking   28

Olives and onions and peppers with liver on skewers   38

Olives, cold spaghetti salad with anchovies and   3

Olykoeks   21

Omelette, herb   36

Omlettes   36

Onion griddle cakes   38

Onion Sandwich   31

Onion sauce, pig's trotters with ...   28

Onions and peppers and olives with liver on skewers

Onions, stuffed   29

Onions with vinegar   35

Opera creams or centers   42

Orange and ginger water ice   18

Orange and quince pie   32

Orange cream filling   39

Orange cream pie   41

Orange fruit soup   38

Orange icing, luscious   41

Orange icing, quick   39

Orange icing, seven-minute   41

Orange jelly   36

Orange lemon custard filling   39

Orange, Bavarois à l'...   9

Orange-filled cake   41

Orange-marmalade drops

Ortiz, Elisabeth Lambert, The Book of Latin American Cooking   8

Otherwise   34

Oxtail with prunes and corn-meal fritters   18

Oyster sauce, sliced steak in   5

-P-

Paglia e fieno alla ghiotta
9

Pan-broiled, soufflé or puffed potatoes   40

Pancakes, griddle or batter cakes   39

Pancakes, Austrian (or nockerlin)

Pancakes, buttermilk
31

Pancakes, cornmeal
38

Pancakes, cottage cheese (or blintzes)   39

Pancakes, French

Pancakes, French stuffed

Pancakes, fruit

Pancakes, German (or pfannkukchen)

Pancakes, Henri Thiele's German   31

Pancakes, potato   40

Pancakes, Russian raised (or blini)   39

Pancakes, sour milk

Pannequaiques   21

Papas y chile verde, sopa di
33

Papashivily, Helen and George, and the editors of Time-Life Books, The Cooking of Russia   26

Paradicsomsalát   4

Paper   12, 18, 33, 34

Paradise or fresh fruit crisp
40

Parcha, Bandhgobi   4

Parfaits, Ice Cream, Sorbets, Frozen Yogourts, Parfaits, Bombes and More, Shona Crawford Poole   18

Parmesan, cauliflower

Parmagiana di Melanzane
11

Parsley butter, cauliflower

Party dinner ... menus
37, 38

Paste, almond or filbert
43

Pastel de pescado económico   32

Pastry, choux for cream buns or éclairs   37

Pastry filling, custard cream or crème patissière   39

Pastry for pie crust   21

Pâte brisée or Muerbeteig or pâte sucrée   41

Pâte feuilletée or puff paste
42

Pâte sucrée or pâte brisée or muerbeteig   41

Pâté, liver   38

Pattern   12

Peach chutney, Albemarle
21

Peach cobbler

Peach or apple or plum cake cockaigne   40

Peach pie   42

Peaches, spiced in brandy
21

Peaches, sweet pickled

Peanut-butter cookies
41

Peanut-butter honey icing, quick

Pearl-tapioca pudding
42

Pears, ginger   21

Pecan drop cookies
41

Pecan or angel slices

Pecan or benne wafers

Pecan or tan or brown sugar kisses   30

Pecan or walnut toasted filling   39

Pecan pie   40

Pecan puffs   41

Pellegrini, Angelo M., James P. Shenton, Dale Brown, Israel Shenker, Peter Wood and the editors of Time-Life Books, American Cooking: The Melting Pot   24

Pencil   25

Pencilled   25, 26, 33

Penne col sugo di cavolfiore
3

Penne con spinaci e ricotta
3

Peperonata   11

Pepper and egg tarts, Basque

Pepper, Spanish ... soup continued

Peppermint cream wafers
43

Peppers and onions and olives with liver on skewers
38

Peppers, green in oil with tomatoes and aubergines continued

Pescado, ensalada de 33

Pesce alla griglia 28

Pesce in cartoccio

Pesce, cappelletti di ... col sugo di gamberetti continued 3

Pesce, espada al salmoriglio

Pesce o carne tra i due piatti

Petit salé 27

Petit salé aux champignons 28

Petit salé au choux 27

Petit salé au poireaux 28

Petit salé aux champignons

Petit salé aux petits pois 27

Petit salé aux pois secs

Petit salé aux pommes 28

Petits pois au lard 27

Petits pois with petit salé

Petits navets sautes en garniture 29

Pfannkukchen or German pancakes 39

Pfeffernüsse 40

Piano 7

Pickled jerusalem artichokes 21

Pickled peaches, sweet

Pickles and chutneys 22

Pickles, carrot 21

Pickles, watermelon rind

Picnic, Claudia Rodin 13

Picnic or lunch box or tea sandwiches 21

Pie, apple

Pie, apple or peach or plum cake cockaigne 40

Pie, apricot or prune

Pie, Aztec 33

Pie, berry with fresh fruit 42

Pie, butterscotch 41

Pie, cherry or berry with frozen fruit 42

Pie, cherry with cooked fruit

Pie, chocolate 40

Pie, chocolate cream

Pie, chocolate-topped custard

Pie, coffee (or tarts) 41

Pie, cream or custard 40

Pie crust flour paste

Pie crust hot-water

Pie crust, pastry for 21

Pie crust, quick and easy 41

Pie crust, rich egg

Pie crust wheatless

Pie, custard caramel 40

Pie, custard or cream

Pie, fresh cherry 42

Pie, German cherry

Pie, glazed fruit

Pie, gravel or crumb 40

Pie, Jefferson Davis

Pie, Key lime 21

Pie, large meat 35

Pie, leek 13

Pie, lemon meringue 21

Pie, mock mince

Pie or cake, bakers' cheese 41

Pie or cake, Boston cream

Pie or cake, ricotta cheese

Pie or tarts, coffee

Pie, orange and quince 32

Pie, orange cream 41

Pie peach 42

Pie, pecan 40

Pie, prune or apricot

Pie, pumpkin or squash

Pie, quince and orange 32

Pie, raised, Jane Grigson's 13

Pie, raisin 49

Pie, raspberry or strawberry

Pie, ricotta cheese 37

Pie, sour cream cherry 42

Pie, transparent 40

Piedmont 28

Pieds de porc vinaigrette

Pies and tarts 32

Pig's trotters with onion sauce 28

Pilot Fish 7

Pineapple apricot conserve 31

Pineapple baked 42

Pineapple liqueur 32

Pineapple sauce or apple or prune or apricot cookies 30

Pinwheel refrigerator cookies 41

Pipérade basquaise 11

Pite, chocolate, latticed 10

Pizza di scarola continued 3

Pizza Margherita

Pizzaiola 32

Plastic 12, 23, 25, 26, 33

Plum blossom and snow 18

Plum or apple or peach pie cockaigne 40

Plum pudding baked

Plumb pudding, frozen 21

Plum bombs 41

Plums in wine jelly 21

Poached ground-cherries 31

Poached or boiled fish 36

Pocket Beer Guide, Michael Jackson 10

Poireaux, petit salé au 28

Poires meringuées au sabayon 29

Pois secs, petit salé aux 27

Poivrons et riz, courgettes farcies 29

Poivrons provençale, salade de

Polenta con burro e formaggio 9

Polenta col gorgonzola

Polenta fritta

Pomiane, Edouard de, Cooking with Pomiane 13

Pommes Anna continued 29

Pommes de terre au lard 28

Pommes de terre sarladaise

Pommes de terre, gallette au fromage

Pommes duchesse 29

Pommes duchesse continued

Pommes soufflées calvados

Pommes soufflées calvados continued

Pommes, petit salé aux 28

Pomodoro piccante, umido di gamberi ai ...

Pompano 7

Pompano en papillote 42

Poole, Shona Crawford, Ice Cream, Sorbets, Frozen Yogourts, Parfaits, Bombes and More 18

Popovers 31

Poppy seed custard torte 41

Porc, côtes de, sautées à la Gasconne 28

Porc, côtes de, à la Bayonnaise

Porc, côtes de, à la charcutiere

Porc, côtes de, au vin blanc

Porc, pieds de, vinaigrette

Pork and watercress soup 5

Pork cake 30

Pork, sweet and sour 5

Potato and ham cakes with eggs 38

Potato cake, chocolate or chocolate caramel

Potato cups, stuffed 40

Potato pancakes

Potatoes Anna

Potatoes, franconia or browned 37, 40

Potatoes, grated 40

Potatoes, hashed brown

Potatoes, lyonnaise

Potatoes, or puffed or pan-broiled or soufflé

Potatoes, tiny new sautéed 40

Poultry 5

Poultry continued 7

Pozole, hearty dinner 33

Preserves six-minute strawberry 31

Preserves, strawberry sunshine

Preserves, tomato 21

Pretzels, almond 30, 42

Prised apart 29

Prosciutto, figs with 31

Prosciutto, melon and figs wrapped in 43

Prune and spiced chocolate cake 42

Prune or apple or apricot or pineapple sauce cookies 30

Prune or apricot Betty 42

Prune or apricot pie 30

Prune or fig or date bars 40

Prune or lemon filling

Prune whip 30

Prunes, clafouti 29

Prunes, flan aux

Prunes with oxtail and cornmeal fritters 18

Pudding, cottage 42

Pudding, apricot 36

Pudding, baked fig 42

Pudding, baked plum

Pudding, bread with meringue

Pudding, Charleston 30

Pudding, coconut 17

Pudding, colonial cheese 31

Pudding, Elizabeth Borton de Treviño's best 17

Pudding, frozen plum 21

Pudding, pearl-tapioca 42

Pudding, steamed sponge 17

Pudding, the Coach House bread and butter 30

Pudding, vanilla

Puddings, queen of 17

Puff paste or pâte feuilletée 42

Puffed or pan-broiled or soufflé potatoes 40

Pumpkin, American baked 11

Pumpkin, babka made with 37

Pumpkin or squash pie 40

Pumpkin or squash soup, East Craftsbury 11

Pumpkin or squash spice cake 37

Pumpkin, fried

Pumpkin, roast

Punch, Roman 21

Purée freneuse 29

Purée, brabant 10

Purée, roast garlic and white bean 43

Puréed vegetable and beef soup 35

-Q-

Quality 33

Queen of puddings 17

Queso asadero, ensalada de 33

Quick and easy pie crust 41

Quick brown sugar icing

Quick cheese dumplings 38

Quick cherry crunch 40

Quick chocolate icing 39

Quick chocolate oil cake 38

Quick decorative icing or Swiss meringue or royal glaze 39

Quick honey peanut-butter icing

Quick lemon icing

Quick maple icing

Quick oatmeal cookies

Quick orange icing

Quick spice oil cake 38

Quick white icing 39

Quick white oil cake 38

Quick-fried crab in aromatic oil 5

Quick-fried sweet and sour spare ribs

Quince and orange pie 32

-R-

Rabbit, caraway macaroni 17

Rabbit, Mexican

Rabbit, tomato

Raised doughnuts 31

Raised dumplings or dampfnudeln 40

Raised pie, Jane Grigson's 13

Raisin or fig or almond filling 39

Raisin pie   40

Rama Rau, Santha and the editors of Time-Life Books, The Cooking of India 22

Raphael, Chaim (introduces) The Jewish Manual edited by a Lady

Raspberries, sliced rounds of honeydew melon filled with 38

Raspberry or strawberry pie 42

Raspberry rum or trifle cake 41

Ravigote sauce, hot 38

Ravioli

Ravioli filling

Ravioli or tortellini with chicken soup   43

Raw apple bread or cake 30

Ray, Elizabeth (editor), The Best of Eliza Acton   6

Reading   31

Recipes: American Cooking 23

Recipes: American Cooking: The Melting Pot   24

Recipes: The Cooking of India   22

Recipes: The Cooking of Italy, Margaret Costa 24

Recipes: The Cooking of Russia   26

Recipes: The Cooking of Vienna's Empire   27

Red devil's food cake 30

Red hominey stew from Jalisco   7

Red hot cauliflower   11

Red mullet   7

Red mullet, with garlic (small)   36

Red salmon   42

Red velvet cake   30

Refrigerator cookies, butter-scotch   41

Refrigerator cookies, chocolate

Refrigerator cookies, pinwheel

Refrigerator cookies, vanilla

Refrigerator lace cookies

Rice and cheese avocados 17

Rice chicken or barley soup 43

Rice cornmeal griddle cakes   38

Rice flour griddle cakes

Rich egg pie crust   41

Rich Meat and Vegetable Soup   36

Rich roll cookies   41

Ricotta cheese pie   37

Ricotta cheese pie or cake 41

Ricotta chocolate filling 39

Ricotta, penne con spinaci e ...   3

Riso, la "Turta" di spinaci e 12

Rissoles or turnovers, sweet 40

River Cafe Cook, Rose Gray and Ruth Rogers   10

Rivera, Guadalupe and Marie-Pierre Colle, Frida's Fiestas: Recipes and Reminiscences of Life with Frida Kahlo. Translator (text), Kenneth Krabbenhoft, translator (recipes), Olga Rigsby   7

Riz et poivron, courgettes farcies

Roast figs (Mrs Crowen's)

Rocks or fruit drop cookies

Roden, Claudia, A book of Middle Eastern Food 35

Roden, Claudia, The Book of Jewish Food: An Odyssey from Samarkand to New York   19

Roden, Claudia, The Cooking of the Middle East: A Sainsbury Cookbook 20

Rodin, Claudia, Picnic 13

Roe and milt, about 42

Rogers, Ruth and Rose Gray, River Cafe Cook Book Easy 10

Roghni nan   4

Roghni roti

Roll cookies   41

Rolled cookies   30

Rolls, clover leaf   23

Roman punch   21

Rombauer, Irma S., Marion Rombauer Becker and Ethan Becker, Joy of Cooking   43

Root, Waverly and the editors of Time-Life Books, The Cooking of Italy   24

Roti, roghni   4

Roulade Léontine or chocolate roll continued   30

Royal glaze or Swiss meringue or quick decorative icing   39

Rubinstein, Helga, The Chocolate Book   33

Rucked covering   23, 25

Rum or bourbon or sherry or brandy balls or walnut spirit balls   30

Rum, hot buttered   38

Rum, raspberry cake or trifle   41

Russian borshch continued   11

Russian raised pancakes or blini

Russian salad   21

Rye bread   31

-S-

Sachertorte   41

Salad, brain   35

Salad, cauliflower and green bean

Salad, cold spaghetti with anchovies and olives   3

Salad, crab meat, tomatoes stuffed with   37

Salad, mixed green with French dressing   38

Salad, Russian   21

Salad, tahina cream   35

Salade de poivrons provençale   29

Salaman, Rena, The Cooking of Greece and Turkey: A Sainsbury Cookbook   37

Salmon sandwich   31

Salmon steaks, broiled or darnes   42

Salmon, cold glazed   42

Salmon, red   42

Salpiçon of fruits   21

Salsa de pan frito   32

Salsa Muselina

Salsicce coi fagioli dall'occhio   9

Saltsa domata   12

Salted almonds   8

Samak blehat   35

Samak malhi   36

Samak malhi bi khall wa rahshi   36

Samak, Shorbet el

Samak Tarator

Sand tarts   30, 42

Sandbakelse   30

Sandwich, anchovy   31

Sandwich, cheese

Sandwich, cottage cheese

Sandwich, cucumber

Sandwich, egg

Sandwich, loaves   38

Sandwich, onion

Sandwich, salmon   31

Sandwich, sardine

Sandwich, submarine or sub or hero or grinder

Sandwich, tomato

Sandwich, tuna fish

Sandwiches, dainty

Sandwiches, lobster or shrimp or crab meat

Sandwiches, tea or lunch box or picnic

Sandwiches, zoo   38

Saraghine alla brace   3

Sardine sandwich

Sardines in the Algerian manner   26

Sauce, apple   21

Sauce, apple... cake   30

Sauce, basic tomato   32

Sauce, bolognese   9

Sauce, chocolate, with lobster   24

Sauce, cranberry   21

Sauce, cranberry (or jelly)   38

Sauce, dipping for raw vegetables, Tuscan   43

Sauce, fried fish with cousbareia ...   36

Sauce, Henri's butter for crêpes Suzettes   39

Sauce, lemon-nutmeg, apple soufflé with 17

Sauce, marchand de vin with fillet of beef 37

Sauce, onion with pig's trotters 28

Sauce, pineapple ... cookies

Sauce, pizzaiola 32

Sauce, ravigote 38

Sauce, tomato basic

Sauce, zemino for fried fish 36

Sauces, making in your Magimix food processor 12

Sauces, meat and fish 25

Saucisse de thann 32

Saucisse de Toulouse

Saucisses de Strasbourg

Sauerkraut, stuffed whole cabbage with 24

Sausage 37

Sausage and macaroni casserole 15

Sausage, Leoni 32

Sausages with cocktails 30

Sayyadiah 36

Scad 7

Scarola, pizza di 3

Scarred 12

Schwartz, Oded, In Search of Plenty: A History of Jewish Food 8

Sciaenid fish 7

Scotch eggs 30

Scotch shortbread 30, 42

Scotch shortbread

Scott, Malkanthi, a letter from 14

Scrambled eggs with vinegar 36

Sea-foam icing, seven-minute 41

Seafood: A Connoisseur's Guide and Cookbook, Alan Davidson and Charlotte Knox

Secrets of the Master Chefs of China, by the editors of *China Pictorial* 22

Seekhi Baingan 4

Separate 32

Separated from 27

Seven-minute lemon icing 41

Seven-minute orange icing

Seven-minute sea-foam icing

Seven-minute white icing

Sharply turned under 11

Sheet cake filled with apples 10

Shenker, Israel, Dale Brown, James P. Shenton, Angelo M. Pellegrini, Peter Wood and the editors of Time-Life Books, American Cooking: The Melting Pot 24

Shenton, James P., Angelo M. Pellegrini, Dale Brown, Israel Shenker, Peter Wood and the editors of Time-Life Books, American Cooking: The Melting Pot

Sherry or bourbon or rum or brandy balls or walnut spirit balls 30

Shorbet el Samak 36

Shortbill spearfish 42

Shortbread, Scotch, 30, 42

Shortcake, blueberry 21

Shortcake, strawberry

Shrimp or lobster or crab meat sandwiches 31

Shurtleff, William and Akiko Aoyagi, The Book of Tofu: Food for Mankind 15

Sicilian style, cauliflower in the ... 11

Sieu ngaap jook 5

Simca's Cuisine, Simone Beck 4

Simple muffins 31

Six-minute strawberry preserves 31

Skillet or upside-down cake 40

Skordalia 12

Sliced rounds of honeydew melon filled with raspberries 38

Sliced steak in oyster sauce 5

Slices, pecan or angel 41

Slight staining 37

Slightly crumpled 7

Slightly damaged 22

Slightly soiled 24, 25, 26, 27, 34

Slightly stained 24

Slimming with Magimix,
Marika Hanbury Tenison
16

Slip   18

Slump   21

Small, blotch   22

Small fish, grilled or deep-fried   36

Small red mullet with garlic

Small stain

Small triangular piece

Small, Marvin, The World's Best Recipes   6

Smith's, Michael, cauliflower soup

Snaps, brandy   41

Snaps, ginger   42

Snickerdoodles   30

Snow and plum blossom 18

Soft centre fondant 42

Soiled   23, 24,25, 26, 27, 28, 30, 37

Sopa de Fideo   33

Sopa de melón escribe

Sopa de papas y chile verde

Sopa de tortilla

Sorbet au cacao   24

Sorbet, blackcurrant 18

Sorbets, Ice Cream, Sorbets, Frozen Yogourts, Parfaits, Bombes and More, Shona Crawford Poole   18

Soufflé amaretto   24

Soufflé, apple with lemon-nutmeg sauce   17

Soufflé, chocolate 30

Soufflé, lemon   17

Soufflé or puffed or pan-broiled potatoes 40

Soufflé Rothschild   17

Soup, Armenian meat soup with burghul   36

Soup, beef and puréed vegetable   35

Soup, brussel sprout 10

Soup casserole, tuna, noodle and mushroom 38

Soup, chicken noodle 43

Soup, chicken rice or barley

Soup, chicken with ravioli or tortellini

Soup, cockaigne fruit

Soup, cold cucumber and yoghourt   35

Soup, Michael Smith's cauliflower continued 11

Soup, East Craftsbury pumpkin or squash

Soup, ful nabbed   35

Soup, fruit   38

Soup, haricot bean   35

Soup, lentil

Soup, matzo ball   43

Soup, meat ball   36

Soup, orange fruit   38

Soup, pork and watercress 5

Soup, pumpkin or squash, East Craftsbury   11

Soup, rich meat and vegetable   36

Soup, Spanish garlic with eggs   43

Soup, Spanish pepper continued   11

Soup, spinach and lentil 3

Soup, squash or pumpkin, East Craftsbury   11

Soup, Turkish spinach 35

Soup, Turkish yoghourt

Soup, yellow split pea

Soup, youghourt and cucumber

Sour cream with brown sugar and grapes   31

Sour cream cake   38

Sour cream cheesecake 41

Sour cream cherry pie 42

Sour milk pancakes   39

Sour-sweet aubergine Spanish style   11

Sources   31

Spaghetti alla Nursina continued   3

Spaghetti salad with anchovies and olives, cold 3

Spaghettini alle vongole 8

Spaghettini con le melanzane

Spanaci, torta di   12

Spanish garlic soup with eggs   43

Spanish pepper soup continued   11

Spare ribs, barbecued   5

Spare ribs, sweet and sour quick-fried

Spearfish, shortbill   42

Speculatius   41

Spekulaas   30

Spice angel cake, high altitude   39

Spice cake, hurry-up   38

Spice, oil cake, quick ...

Spice cake, spiced chocolate with citron   42

Spice velvet cake

Spiced chocolate and prune cake

Spiced, crab apples   21

Spiced cranberry jelly   38

Spiced peaches in brandy   21

Spices, Salt and Aromatics in the English Kitchen, Elizabeth David   8

Spinach and lentil soup   35

Spinach, creamed   15

Soup and lentil   35

spinaci e riso, la "Turta" di   12

spinaci, penne con ricotta e ...   3

spinaci, torta di   12

Spiral   16, 22, 23, 24, 26, 27

Split, book ... in two   4, 5

Split pea soup, yellow   35

Sponge cake, high altitude   39

Sponge layer or ... roll or roulade Léontine   30

Sponge pudding, steamed   17

Spring and winter greens   11

Springerle   42

Spritz or cookie-press cookies   41

Squares and bars, about   40

Squash or pumpkin pie   40

Squash or pumpkin soup, East Craftsbury   11

Squash, spice or pumpkin cake   30

Stain, small   23

Stained   passim

Stained and torn   3, 32, 37, 42

Stained with oil   42

Staining   17, 37

Stains, other minor not recorded   43

Stars, cinnamon   39

Steak, sliced in oyster sauce   5

Steamed sponge pudding   17

Stew, red hominey from Jalisco   7

Stick candy cookies   30

Sticker   12, 23, 25, 33

Sticky yellow slip   20, 29

Stir-fried, Chinese leaf

Stock, beetroot

Stoneground   33

Strawberries and cream   32

Strawberries Romanoff   38

Strawberry jam, sun-cooked   21

Strawberry or raspberry pie   42

Strawberry preserves, six-minute   31

Strawberry preserves, sunshine

Strawberry shortcake   21

Stuck   29, 32

Strudel, continued   38

Stuffed aubergine slices with cream cheese   35

Stuffed baked artichokes   37

Stuffed eggplant with cheese   15

Stuffed French pancakes or crêpes   39

Stuffed morels   10

Stuffed onions   29

Stuffed potato cups   40

Stuffed tomatoes   32

Stuffed vine leaves, cold

Stuffed vine leaves, hot 35

Stuffed whole cabbage with sauerkraut 24

Stuffed zucchini 29

Sub or hero or grinder or submarine sandwich 31

Submarine or sub or hero or grinder sandwich

Substituted 32

Sugar and sour cream, grapes with

Sugar drop cookies with oil

Sugo di gamberetti, cappelletti di pesci col continued 3

Summer Cooking, Elizabeth David 20

Sun-cooked strawberry jam

Sunshine strawberry preserves 31

Supplement 43

Swedish limpa

Sweet and sour pork 5

Sweet and sour spare ribs

Sweet chocolate cake 30

Sweet chocolate or chocolate chunk or chocolate chip or Toll House cookies 30

Sweet pickled peaches 21

Sweet turnovers or rissoles 40

Sweetened whipped cream or crème Chantilly fillings

Sweet-sour aubergine Spanish style 11

Swiss meringue or royal glaze or quick decorative icing 39

-T-

Ta'amia or falafel 35

Tacos 33

Taquitos

Tagliatelle alla bolognese 9

Tahina bi hummus 35

Tahina bil fessih

Tahina cream salad

Tagine malsouka

Tamattar Bhurta 4

Tan or brown sugar or pecan kisses 30

Tandori-style chicken 10

Taneja, Meera, New Indian Cooking 9

Taramasalata 35

Tarte, cream meringue cockaigne

Tartelletes 40

Tarts and pies 32

Tarts and tartlets for canapés 38

Tarts or pie, coffee 40

Tarts, apple 42

Tarts, Banbury

Tarts, chess

Tarts, courgette 13

Tarts (or flan) custard with fruit 40

Tarts, egg and pepper, Basque 11

Tarts, individual nut 41

Tarts, macaroon jam

Tarts, sand 30, 42

Tattered cover(s) 9, 20, 33, 37

Tattered dust jacket 19

Tea or lunch box or picnic sandwiches 31

Tea wafers 39

Tenison, Marika Hanbury, Slimming with Magimix 16

Tenison Marika Hanbury, The Magimix and Food Processor Cookery Book 12

Tenison, Marika Hanbury, The Magimix Food Preparation Machine Information, Instruction & Recipe Book 16

The Alice B. Toklas Cook Book, Alice B. Toklas 27

The American Heritage Cookbook, Helen McNulty (recipes editor), Eleanor Noderer (associate recipes editor), Helen Duprey Bullock (historical foods consultant) 21

The Bean Book, Rose Elliot 6

The Best of Eliza Acton, Elizabeth Ray (editor)

The Book of Jewish Food: An Odyssey from Samarkand to New York, Claudia Roden 19

The Book of Latin American Cooking, Elisabeth Lambert Ortiz 8

The Book of the Sausage, Antony and Araminta Hippisley Coxe 32

The Book of Tofu: Food for Mankind, William Shurtleff and Akiko Aoyagi 15

The Chinese Cookbook, Craig Claiborne and Virginia Lee 17

The Chocolate Book, Helga Rubinstein 33

The Classic Italian Cookbook, Marcella Hazan 8

The Coach House bread and butter pudding 30

The Cooking of Greece and Turkey: A Sainsbury Cookbook, Rena Salaman 37

The Cooking of India, Santha Rama Rau and the editors of Time-Life Books 22

The Cooking of Italy, Waverly Root 24

The Cooking of Russia, Helen and George Papashvily and the editors of Time-Life Books 26

The Cooking of the Middle East: A Sainsbury Cookbook, Claudia Roden 20

The Cooking of Vienna's Empire, Joseph Wechsberg and the editors of Time-Life Books 26

The Country Kitchen, Jocasta Innes 22

The Cuisine of Hungary, George Lang 10

The Food and Cooking of Russia, Lesley Chamberlain 6

The foods we eat continued 37

The foods we heat 38

The Guardian book service 10

The Jewish Manual: Information on Jewish and Modern Cookery with a Collection of Valuable Recipes and Hints Relating to the Toilette edited by a Lady, introduction by Chaim Raphael 13

The Joy of Chinese Cooking, Doreen Yen Hung Feng 5

The Magimix and Food Processor Cookery Book, Marika Tenison Hanbury 12

The Magimix Food Preparation Machine Information, Instruction & Recipe Book, Marika Hanbury Tenison 16

The Mushroom Feast, Jane Grigson 7

The New York Times Cookbook, Craig Claiborne 17

The Rituals of Dinner, Margaret Visser 15

The Second Classic Italian Cookbook, Marcella Hazan 3

The Settlement Cookbook: The way to a Man's Heart 15

The South African Culinary Tradition with 167 Authentic Recipes, Renata Coetzee 25

The Sunday Times Guide to the World's Best Food, Michael Bateman, Caroline Conran, Oliver Gillie 25

The World's Best Recipes, Marvin Small 6

Thins, butter 41

Thins, ginger 40

Three-minute icing 39

Tian de courgettes au riz 29

Timbale de courgettes

Timbales, chicken liver

Tiny new potatoes sautéed 40

Title page inscription 12

Toasted walnut or pecan filling 39

Toklas, Alice B., The Alice B. Toklas Cook Book 27

Toll house cookies or sweet chocolate or chocolate chunk or chocolate chip 30

Tom and Jerry in quantity 38

Tomato ketchup 21

Tomato preserves

Tomato rabbit

Tomato relish, Yankee

Tomato sandwich 31

Tomato sauce, basic 32

Tomato, duck with 10

Tomatoes and basil with bruschetta 43

Tomatoes, aubergines and green peppers in oil continued

Tomatoes, stuffed 32

Tomatoes stuffed with crab meat salad 37

Tonno in agrodolce alla trapanese 3

Tonno, zucchini ripiene di 12

Toppings, meringue 38

Torn, area ... out 12

Torn cover 32

Torn dust jacket 3, 13

Torn fragment 32

Torn out almost completely 12

Torn page 25, 27, 37

Torn pages 29, 37

Torn paper 37

Torn spine 11, 30

Torn unevenly

Torta di spinaci continued 12

Torte chocolate walnut 41

Torte, chocolate date

Torte, custard poppy seed

Tortelettes

Tortellini or ravioli with chicken soup 43

Tortilla, sopa di 33

Tortillas

Tourte Limousine 29

Transparent food-bag 11

Transparent pie 40

Triffle or raspberry rum cake

Trippa alla parmigiana 9

Trotters, pig's with onion sauce 28

Trout, grilled 21

Tsimmes 18

Tuna fish sandwich 31

Tuna with avocado purée 35

Tuna, noodle and mushroom soup casserole 38

Turkish spinach soup 35

Turkish yoghourt soups

Turlu 36

Turnovers or rissoles, sweet 40

Turrcarri kahsta, mhaans 4

Turrcarri sadah, mhaans

Turrcarri bandhgobi

Turrcarri gurdakupura

Tuscan dipping sauce for raw vegetables 43

Tutmaj 35

Two-egg cake, high altitude 39

Tyropitta 35

-U-

Uborkasaláta 4

Umido di gamberi al pomodoro piccante 3

Uncooked fondant 42

Uncooked frozen jams

Unidentified 32

Upside-down or skillet cake 40

Upside-down chocolate cake 30

Uskumru dolmasu 36

-V-

Vanilla pudding 30

Vanilla refrigerator cookies 41

Vegetable and meat, rich soup 36

Vegetable, puréed and beef soup

Vegetables raw, Tuscan dipping sauce for 43

Vegetables with braised liver 38

Vegetarian Dishes from the Middle East, Arto der Haroutunian 15

Velvet spice cake 42

Very serious staining 17

Vienna pastry 41

Vienna's empire 26, 27

Vine leaves, stuffed, cold 35

Vine leaves, stuffed, hot 35

Vinegar 35, 36

Visser, Margaret, The Rituals of Dinner 15

Vongole con spaghettini 8

Vongole, zuppa di, vellutata 9

-W-

Wafers peppermint cream 43

Wafers, benne or pecan 41

Wafers, jubilee

Wafers, leaf 39

Wafers, molasses nut 41

Wafers, nut

Wafers, nut curled

Wafers, tea

Waffles 31

Waffles 38

Walnut chocolate torte 41

Walnut or pecan toasted filling 39

Walnut spirit balls or bourbon or sherry or rum 30

Wara einab 35

Wassail 38

Water ice, orange and ginger 18

Watercress, pork and ... soup 5

Watermelon rind pickles

Wechsberg, Joseph and the editors of Time-Life Books, The Cooking of Vienna's Empire 26

Weir, Robin and Caroline Liddell, Ices: The Definitive Guide 18

Welsh lamb with laver 11

Wheatless pie crust 41

Whip 30

Whipped cream cake 38

Whipped cream sweetened or crème Chantilly fillings

Whipped cream cheese-cake 41

White bean and roast garlic purée 43

White beans

White beans, browned-in-the-oven 27

White cake, high altitude 39

White boiled icing 41

White icing, quick 38

White icing, seven-minute 41

Whitings, King 28

Whole dog eared 18

Whole-grain bread 31

Whole-grain griddle cakes 39

Whole-wheat bread, good 31

Wild 16

Wine jelly, plums in 21

Winter and spring greens 11

Wood, Peter, Israel Shenker, Dale Brown, James P. Shenton, Angelo M. Pellegrini, and the editors of Time-Life Books, American Cooking: The Melting Pot 24

Wrasse, Corkwing 7

Wrasse, Cuckoo

Wrasse, kindred fish and ...

Wrinkled 18, 28

-X-

-Y-

Yang chow Haah Kow 5

Yankee tomato relish 21

Yeast coffee cake 37

Yellow split pea soup 35

Yellow sticky slip 20, 29

Yellowing 26

Yoghourt, aubergines fried with ... 35

Yoghourt, cold cucumber soup and

Yogourts, Frozen, Ice Cream, Sorbets, Parfaits, Bombes and More, Shona Crawford Poole 18

Yolk cookies 42

Yook, hoong sieu juh 7

Yuan Mei, her bêche-de mer gourmet

-Z-

Zemino sauce for fried fish 36

Zoo sandwiches 38

Zucchini 8

Zucchini frite con fettuccine 3

Zucchini ripiene di tonno 12

Zucchini, stuffed 29

Zuppa di vongole vellutata 9

Zwieback or graham cracker or ginger snap crust 42

8 stoneground corn tortillas 33

88 Danish Dishes, Hetna Dedichen 3

End

Printed in the United Kingdom
by Lightning Source UK Ltd.
111094UKS00001B/3

www.ingramcontent.com/pod-product-compliance
Lightning Source LLC
Chambersburg PA
CBHW030914180526
45163CB00004B/1824